Clan Fraser

A history celebrating over 800 years of the Family in Scotland

Flora Marjory Fraser
20th Lady Saltoun

SCOTTISH CULTURAL PRESS
EDINBURGH

First published 1997 by
Scottish Cultural Press
Unit 14, Leith Walk Business Centre,
130 Leith Walk, Edinburgh EH6 5DT
Tel: 0131 555 5950 • Fax: 0131 555 5018
e-mail: scp@sol.co.uk

British Library Cataloguing in Publication Data
A catalogue entry for this book is available from the British Library

ISBN: 1 84017 010 7 (hardback)
ISBN: 1 84017 005 0 (paperback)

Printed and bound by
Cromwell Press, Melksham, Wiltshire

Clan Fraser

A history

The Lady Saltoun, Chief of Clan Fraser, with
her eldest daughter, Kate [The Hon. Mrs Nicolson],
and her grandson, Master Alexander Fraser,
in the garden at Cairnbulg Castle, Fraserburgh

Conversation Piece

L-R: General Sir David Fraser, the present Lady Saltoun, the late Lady Saltoun, the Master of Saltoun who was killed serving in the Grenadier Guards in World War II, the late Lord Saltoun, and their dog, grouped round the tea table in the Great Hall

by Frederick Elwell, 1942

Table of Contents

Introduction

So many people over the years have asked so many questions about the history of the family and clan, that I thought it was time to write a booklet which would answer at least some of those questions, and that is what this is intended to do. It is not intended to be a comprehensive history of the family. To write such a book would take years of patient research, and, alas! I do not have time for that, interesting as it would be, and much as I should love to do it.

The Frasers of Philorth, my line, have very few known cadet branches extant. In fact, my great grandfather, the 17th Lord Saltoun, who wrote a very scholarly and well researched history of them about 120 years ago, said that apart from his brothers and his children, his nearest Fraser relations were the Lovats! A few years ago, I discovered a branch in Finland, and I'm sure there must be others, but we do not know of them. In contrast, the Lovat line has a great many cadet branches, many of which were prolific. Ten or twelve children in a family was not uncommon. Although the Lovats never cleared their people from the Glens to make way for sheep, there was small prospect of advancement in life for younger sons unless they went south to one of the cities or emigrated, which is what many of them did. Some went to Edinburgh, Glasgow or London, many went to America, Canada, Australia or New Zealand and prospered and founded families there, especially in the eighteenth and nineteenth centuries. What is sad is that so few of them seem to have kept records of where in Scotland they came from, and this can make tracing their ancestry rather difficult.

I am greatly indebted to Marie Fraser in Toronto for typing and laying out this book on her computer and for the genealogies which she has computerised from my cousin, General Sir David Fraser's trees of all known branches of the family. Without their help, I could not have done it.

Saltoun

Cairnbulg Castle, Fraserburgh

List of Illustrations

List of Illustrations

1

Brief History of Clan Fraser

Origin of Name Fraser

The Frasers probably came from Anjou in France, and the name probably derives from Fresel or Freseau. Some have suggested that they descend from the tribe called Friselii in Roman Gaul, whose badge was a strawberry plant. The truth of these stories is unknown but it is generally believed that the name Fraser traces its origins to the French provinces of Anjou and Normandy. The French word for strawberry is *fraise* and growers were called *fraisiers*. The Fraser arms are silver strawberry flowers on a field of blue. ***Only the Chief is entitled to use these arms plain and undifferenced.***

Beginning of Clan Fraser

They first appear in Scotland around 1160 when Simon Fraser made a gift of a church at Keith in East Lothian, to the monks at Kelso Abbey. These lands eventually passed to a family who became Earls Marischal of Scotland after adopting Keith as their name. The Frasers moved into Tweeddale in the twelfth and thirteenth centuries and from there into the counties of Stirling, Angus, Inverness and Aberdeen.

About five generations later, Sir Simon Fraser [the Patriot] was captured fighting for Robert the Bruce, and executed with great cruelty by Edward I in 1306. The patriot's line ended in two co-heiresses: the elder daughter married Sir Hugh Hay, ancestor of the Earls of Tweeddale, and the younger daughter married Sir Patrick Fleming, ancestor of the Earls of Wigton.

Sir Andrew Fraser of Touch-Fraser [d. 1297], cousin of the patriot, was the father of Sir Alexander Fraser of Cowie [ancestor of the Frasers of Philorth], Sir Simon Fraser [ancestor of the Frasers of Lovat], Sir Andrew Fraser, and Sir James Fraser of Frendraught, whose line ended with his great granddaughter, Mauld Fraser, who married Alexander Dunbar of Moray. Sir Alexander was killed at the Battle of Dupplin in 1332 and his three younger brothers were killed at the Battle of Halidon Hill in 1333.

Families descended from the early Frasers were of Touch-Fraser, Drumelzier and Hales, Oliver Castle, Cornton, Fruid, Frendraught, Cowie, Forglen and Tulifour. From the family of Fruid descended the Frasers of Daltullich, Dunballoch, Fanellan, Kingillie, Munlochy, Newton, Phopachy and Tain.

Frasers of Philorth - Lords Saltoun

The senior line is descended from Sir Alexander Fraser, who took part in the victory at Bannockburn in 1314. In 1316 he married Robert the Bruce's widowed sister, Lady Mary, who had been imprisoned in a cage by Edward I. Sir Alexanader was appointed Chamberlain of Scotland in 1319, and his seal appears on the letter dated 6th April 1320 to Pope John XXII, seeking recognition of the country's political independence under the kingship of Robert Bruce, which became known as the *Declaration of Arbroath*. He received lands in Aberdeen, Kincardine and Forfar to compensate for the lands confiscated by Edward I in 1306.

His son, Sir William Fraser of Cowie, was killed at the Battle of Durham in 1346, and in 1375 his grandson, Sir Alexander Fraser of Cowie & Durris, acquired the Manor Place (later to become Cairnbulg Castle) and lands of Philorth by marriage with Lady Joanna, younger daughter and co-heiress of the Earl of Ross. According to a prophecy of Thomas the Rhymer: *While a cock craws in the north, there'll be a Fraser at Philorth.*

Several generations later, following the building of the harbour in 1546 by his grandfather, Alexander Fraser, 7th laird of Philorth [c.1495-1569], Sir Alexander Fraser, 8th laird of Philorth [c.1536-1623], had built in 1570 Fraserburgh Castle, later the Kinnaird Head Lighthouse. In doing this he bankrupted himself and had to sell the castle of Philorth, which passed out of the family for over 300 years until the 19th Lord Saltoun bought it back in 1934.

Sir Alexander received from King James VI in 1588 & 1592 charters creating the fishing village of Faithlie, which he had transformed into a fine town and harbour, which he had much improved, into a Burgh of Regality and a Free Port, called Fraser's Burgh, and authorising him to found a University, which was short lived. In 1588 King James VI wrote to ask him for the loan of £1,000, a considerable sum. In 1596, he wrote again:

> *Right Trust Friend, - We greet you heartily well. Hearing that you have a gyirfalcon, which is esteemed to be the best hawk in all that country, and meetest for us that has so good liking of that pastime; we have therefore taken occasion effectuously to request and desire you, seeing hawks are but gifting gear and not otherwise to be accounted between us and you, being so*

> *well and long acquainted, that of courtesy you will bestow on us that your hawk, and send her here to us with this bearer, our servant, whom we have...directed to bring and carry her tenderly. Wherein as you shall report our hearty and special thanks, so shall you find us ready to requite your courtesy and goodwill with no less pleasure in any of the like suits, as occasion shall present. Thus resting persuaded of your pleasuring us hereanent, we commit you in God's protection.*

No doubt he got his hawk!

The 8th laird was succeeded by his eldest son, Alexander Fraser, 9th laird of Philorth [c.1570-1636], who in 1595 married Margaret, heiress of the Abernethies, Lords Saltoun. In 1668 their son Alexander Fraser, 10th of Philorth [1604-1693] also became 10th Lord Saltoun, a title which had belonged to the Abernethy family since 1445. He was severely wounded at the Battle of Worcester in 1651, but survived, thanks to his servant, James Cardno, who rescued him from the battlefield, hid him and nursed him, and got him home to Fraserburgh. In 1666 he built a house about a mile from Fraserburgh which he called Philorth House, where the family lived until it was burnt down in 1915. The family took no part in the Jacobite Rebellions of 1715 and 1745.

The 10th Lord's son and heir, Alexander Fraser, Master of Saltoun [c.1630-1682], married three times, Lady Anne Kerr, Lady Marion Cunningham and Lady Sophia Erskine. The Master died in his father's lifetime, leaving his only surviving son William, by his first wife, to succeed his grandfather.

William Fraser, 11th Lord Saltoun [1654-1714/5] married Margaret Sharp, daughter of the Archbishop of St. Andrew's, who was dragged from his carriage and murdered in front of another of his daughters. Margaret, although not the Archbishop's sole heir, brought a very considerable tocher [dowry] with her. This retrieved the family fortunes, which were in a very bad way after the death of the Master, who was very kindly and not a very good business man!

Following the death in 1696 of Hugh Fraser, 9th Lord Lovat, without male issue, his young widow arranged a marriage for their eldest daugther Amelia with Alexander Fraser, Master of Saltoun, later 12th Lord Saltoun [1685-1748].

When the Master's father, 11th Lord Saltoun, was travelling to Castle Dounie to discuss the details with Lady Lovat, Amelia's uncle, Thomas Fraser of Beaufort and his son Simon, later 11th Lord Lovat, kidnapped him, held him prisoner and threatened to hang him unless he agreed to cancel the proposed marriage, which he did. Therefore, in 1707, the Master of Saltoun married Lady Mary Gordon, daughter of George, 1st Earl of Aberdeen, and her dowry enabled him to restore his family's fortune.

When the 12th Lord Saltoun's second son George was growing up, his father told him that it was time he decided what he wanted to do in life, and asked him whether he had had any thoughts on the matter, to which he answered, *Yes father, I have.* When 12th pressed him on the matter, *Well, George, what have you got in mind?* George replied, *Well, father, I should like to be a tanner.* His father exclaimed, *A TANNER*! *What a ridiculous idea. Why on earth do you want to be a tanner?* George responded, *Well, you see, I should only need two hides, yours and my brother's, and I should be set up for life.* He got them! His elder brother Alexander Fraser, 13th Lord Saltoun [1710-1751] died unmarried, and George succeeded as 14th Lord Saltoun [1720-1781].

Anne Fraser [circa 1719-1807], elder daughter of 12th Lord Saltoun, told the following story:-

The Danish Fleet appeared off Fraserburgh and anchored in the bay. The Admiral and officers were invited to dinner by 12th Lord Saltoun at Fraserburgh Castle. While they were at dinner, a solitary sailor left one of the ships and rowed to the shore at Broadsea. He was sent for and asked by the Admiral why he had left his ship. He replied that the previous night he had dreamt that his wife appeared to him and implored him to leave his ship and get to land, for the following day a violent storm would get up and all the fleet would be sunk and everyone drowned. He dreamt this several times, and it made such an impression on him that he had done as she said. That very afternoon a violent storm did get up and the whole fleet was wrecked and all the sailors drowned, with the exception of himself and the officers who were dining at the castle, who could not get back to their ships, so rapidly did the force of the wind increase.

I believe this disaster is a matter of historical fact. Storms do get up with very great rapidity here. I have known the wind to increase from dead calm to gale-force in a matter of a very few minutes. Anne would have been about 11 years old at the time, so would have remembered the event quite clearly.

The 14th Lord was succeeded by his son, Alexander Fraser, 15th Lord Saltoun [1758-1793] who married Marjory, only daughter and heiress of Simon Fraser of Ness Castle. One day she drove into Fraserburgh in her carriage in order to buy a pair of gloves. The carriage stopped outside the shop, probably the saddler's. She sent the footman in to fetch some gloves for her inspection. After a few minutes, the shopkeeper came out, very nervous and red in the face and handed her a pair of rough coarse leather gloves, suitable for a ploughman. She was somewhat taken aback, but then she looked past the footman into the shop where she could see two familiar figures - her younger sons! So she pulled on the gloves, said to the shopkeeper, *Thank you, these will do perfectly* and drove home.

When King George IV visited Edinburgh in about 1824, a Ball was given. He was very stout and wore a very short kilt with, I believe, flesh coloured tights under it! She attended the Ball and when a friend commented on the shortness of the kilt, she replied, *Well, since we see him so seldom, we may as well see as much as possible of him when we do.*

The 15th Lord died young and was succeeded by his son, Alexander George Fraser, 16th Lord Saltoun [1785-1853]. While attending Eton, he was said to have made history by being the first boy to jump into the River Thames from Windsor Bridge, and at the age of 17 was commissioned into the Army. Later to become a Lieutenant General, he spent most of his time on active service during the Napoleonic Wars. In 1815 he commanded the Light Companies of the First Regiment of Guards [later the Grenadier Guards] in the Orchard at Hougoumont, in the morning of the Battle of Waterloo, and it was he who, later in the day, first noticed the Imperial Guard emerge from the hollow where they had been hiding all day, and drew the Duke of Wellington's attention to them.

His newly married wife, Catherine, had made him a purse, and he had it in his trouser pocket full of gold ducats at the siege of Peronne shortly after Waterloo. He was hit in the thigh by grape-shot with such force that he was knocked over, but the shot buried itself in the coins in the purse, which were all bent and twisted, and he only suffered a nasty bruise. But for it, he would probably have been mortally wounded.

The 16th Lord died without legitimate issue and was succeeded by his nephew, Alexander Fraser, 17th Lord Saltoun [1820-1886], who wrote *The Frasers of Philorth, Lords Saltoun*. In the Preface [written in 1879], he makes the following observation:

> *The representatives of the respective lines of Philorth and Lovat were nearest of kin to each other in 1464, with the exception of the six sons of*

the Philorth of that date; and such has been the extinction of male descendants in the various branches of the line of Philorth, that at the present time, with the exception of my own two sons, my two brothers, and their four sons, numbering eight persons in all, Lord Lovat is my nearest legitimate male connection of the Fraser name.

The 17th Lord was succeeded by his eldest son, Alexander Fraser, 18th Lord Saltoun [1851-1933]. He, in turn, was succeeded by Alexander Arthur Fraser, 19th Lord Saltoun [1886-1979], who followed in his father's footsteps by serving with the Gordon Highlanders, as a captain in the 1st Battalion in the First World War, and was awarded the Military Cross. He was a prisoner of war in Germany for most of the war.

The 19th Lord served as Grand Master Mason for Scotland, and was a Representative Peer for Scotland from 1936 to 1964. At the time of his death in 1979, he had sat in the House of Lords longer than any other living peer. Latterly, he devoted himself to working for the Royal National Lifeboat Institution.

His daughter, Flora Fraser, 20th Lady Saltoun, an active member of the House of Lords, is CHIEF OF THE NAME OF FRASER. An Episcopalian, she is married to Captain Alexander Ramsay of Mar, a great-grandson of Queen Victoria. They have three daughters, of whom the eldest, Kate (The Hon. Mrs. Nicolson) has one son and two daughters.

Families descended from the Philorth line are of Ardglassie, Durris, Findrack, Forglen, Forest, Fraserfield, Hospitalfield, Lonmay, Memsie, Park, Quarrelbuss, Rathilloch, Techmuiry, Tornaveen and Tyrie.

Frasers of Lovat - Lords Lovat

The Frasers of Lovat descend from Sir Simon Fraser [brother of Sir Alexander, the Chamberlain], who married Lady Margaret Sinclair, daughter of the Earl of Caithness. Documents, dated 12th September 1367, connect a Fraser with the lands of Lovat and the Aird. Among the lands acquired by the Lovat Frasers, the prominent ones were in Stratherrick, which was very dear to the hearts of the Lovat chiefs, the church lands of Beauly Priory in Inverness-shire, part of the south shore of Beauly Firth, and the whole of Strathfarrar. Beauly was founded in about 1230 by John Bissett, who also built Lovat Castle. About 1460 Hugh Fraser, 6th of Lovat [c.1436-1501] became the 1st Lord Lovat. He was the son of Thomas Fraser, 5th of Lovat [c.1417-1455] and Lady Janet Dunbar, daughter of Thomas, Earl of Moray.

Several generations later, Hugh Fraser, 9th Lord Lovat [1666-1696], who had four daughters but no son, willed his estates to his grand-uncle, Thomas Fraser of Beaufort [fourth and only surving son of Hugh, 7th Lord Lovat] instead of his eldest daughter Amelia [1686-1763]. Thomas Fraser's second son Simon, later 11th Lord Lovat [1668-1747] had planned to marry the Lovat heiress, Amelia.

When the plan failed, in retaliation, Simon, with his Fraser clansmen besieged Castle Dounie, took possession of the lands, and he forcibly married her mother, the dowager Lady Lovat [1663-1743]. For this lawless behaviour, Simon and his accomplices were tried in 1698 by the Court of Judiciary on a charge of high treason and other offences, and condemned to death. To make matters worse, in 1702 Amelia married her cousin, Alexander Mackenzie, younger of Prestonhall, who assumed the name Fraser of Fraserdale, and the Court decided in favour of her claims to the rights and dignities of her father's house.

These claims were challenged by Thomas Fraser of Beaufort [1631-1699], who eventually assumed the title of 10th Lord Lovat, in succession to his grand-nephew. However, his position was so complicated by the 9th Lord's conflicting testamentary arrangements that he was debarred from possession of the estates, which remained with the latter's daughter Amelia, Lady Lovat.

In the summer of 1702 Simon escaped to France and there began organising a Jacobite Rising in Scotland. Although the house of Lovat had until then followed the tenets of the Reformation, Simon made a new departure by espousing the Roman Catholic faith. However, Simon "The Fox" plotted with both Government and Jacobite forces, his support being given where he thought it most to his advantage. Simon Fraser, 11th Lord Lovat, was the last nobleman to be beheaded on Tower Hill in London on 9th April 1747 for his role in the Jacobite Rebellion that had led to the Battle of Culloden the previous year. The Lovat title was attained by an Act of Parliament and the estates were forfeited to the Crown.

The 11th Lord's eldest son, Simon Fraser, Master of Lovat [1726-1782], was pardoned and raised two regiments: in 1757, the *78th Fraser Highlanders* who fought with Wolfe at Louisbourg and Quebec; and in 1775, the *71st Fraser Highlanders* to serve with the British armies in the American Revolution. He rose to the rank of Lieutenant General, and the forfeited Lovat estates were restored to him in 1774, but not the title.

The Master's younger half-brother, Archibald Campbell Fraser [1736-1815], was Consul General of Algiers in 1776, and in 1794 raised the *Fraser Fencibles* for service during the Irish Rebellion. Colonel Archibald succeeded General Simon in the Lovat estates and in the representation of Inverness-shire in the House of Commons. On his first appearance there in 1782, he played a prominent role in supporting the motion by the

Marquis of Graham, later Duke of Montrose, for the Repeal of the *Unclothing Act* and legalizing the use of the Highland dress.

With the death of Colonel Archibald Campbell Fraser in 1815, without legitimate surviving issue, the original line died out, and the Lovat estates passed to the nearest collateral heir-male, Thomas Alexander Fraser, 10th of Strichen [1802-1875], a distant cousin who was descended from Thomas Fraser of Knockie & Strichen [1548-1612], second son of Alexander Fraser, 4th Lord Lovat [1527-1557] and Janet, daughter of Sir John Campbell of Cawdor. In 1837 he was created Baron Lovat in the Peerage of the United Kingdom, and the attainder of the ancient Scottish title was reversed by an Act of Parliament in his favour in 1857, when he became 14th Lord Lovat.

Alexander Fraser [1860-1936], a native of Inverness-shire who knew him, in *The Clan Fraser in Canada: Souvenir of the First Annual Gathering*, held in Toronto in 1894, noted: *The succession of the Strichen family created a strong hostile feeling among the Clansmen and the old tenants generally, many of them believing that other aspirants who appeared had stronger claims.* There were indeed two other claimants to the Scottish title who presented petitions to the House of Lords. In 1855 the Rev. Alexander Garden Fraser of Beaufort, South Carolina, claimed to be a descendant of Thomas Fraser of Beaufort's third son John; and in 1885 John Fraser of Carnarvon claimed to be a descendant of Thomas Fraser of Beaufort's eldest son Alexander.

Alexander Fraser also related *a curious incident to illustrate the religious beliefs which were held then in the Highlands.* The Rev. Archibald Macdonald in *The Old Lords of Lovat and Beaufort* noted that the 11th Lord Lovat's sons *were educated as Protestants*, even though he had espoused the Roman Catholic faith.

The 14th Lord was for many years Lord-Lieutenant of Inverness. He was succeeded by his eldest son, Simon Fraser, 15th Lord Lovat [1828-1887], who held the same post from 1872 until his death, and commanded the Inverness-shire Militia.

The 15th Lord was succeeded by his second son, Simon Joseph Fraser, 16th Lord Lovat [1871-1933], who served in the 1st Life Guards. In 1899 he raised the Lovat Scouts who fought in the South African War. Major General Lord Lovat commanded the Highland Mounted Brigade in the First World War, and was awarded the Distinguished Service Order.

His eldest son, Brigadier Simon Christopher Joseph Fraser, 17th Lord Lovat [1911-1995], was a legendary Commando leader in the Second World War and, shortly after the D-Day Landing, was severely wounded. He was awarded the Distinguished Service Order and Military Cross. Following the war, he served as Churchill's personal emissary to Stalin in Moscow, before returning to civilian life and becoming a distinguished cattle breeder.

A Roman Catholic, the 17th Lord died on 16th March 1995, aged 83, his eldest son and his youngest having died the previous March. His grandson, Simon Fraser, born in 1977, is the 18th Lord Lovat and 25th *MacShimi*, the CHIEF OF CLAN FRASER OF LOVAT.

The name Lovat means *a swampy plain*. The chiefs are called *MacShimi* which means the son of Simon. Castle Dounie was home of the chiefs of Lovat from 1511 until it was burned following Culloden. Beaufort Castle, built on the site in the 1870s by the 15th Lord Lovat, suffered a bad fire in 1938, which destroyed the picture gallery, ballroom and library. The castle, with contents, was sold in 1995 to Mrs. Ann Gloag as a private home. The Lovat family seat is Beauly, Inverness-shire.

Families of the Lovat line are of Aberchalder, Abersky, Achnagairn, Ardochy, Balnain, Balloan, Belladrum, Boblanie, Bochrubin, Brae, Bught, Castleleather, Cleragh, Clunevackie, Culbokie, Culduthel, Culmiln, Dromdoe, Erchitt, Errogie, Eskadale, Fairfield, Farraline, Fingask, Foyers, Guisachan, Golford, Gortuleg, Inverallochy, Kiltarlity, Kinneries, Knock, Kyllachy, Leadclune, Merkinch, Moniack, Muilzie, Reelig, Ruthven, Strichen, Struy and Teanakyle.

Frasers of Muchalls - Lords Fraser

In 1366 Thomas Fraser, a descendant of Sir Alexander Fraser of Cornton [brother of Sir Richard Fraser of Touch-Fraser], exchanged lands in Petyndreich, Stirlingshire for those of Kinmundy, Aberdeenshire. His grandson Thomas exchanged the estate of Cornton for Stonywood and Muchalls in Aberdeenshire.

His descendant, Andrew Fraser [1574-1636], who was created Lord Fraser by Charles I in 1633, completed Castle Fraser in 1636. The title became extinct following the accidental death in 1716 of Charles, 4th Lord Fraser, a Jacobite, while trying to escape from Government troops.

The 4th Lord died without issue, and his stepson by his wife's first marriage, William Fraser of Inverallochy [c.1672-1716/7], succeeded to the Castle Fraser estates, followed by Charles *Auld Inverallochy* [1701-1787], also a Jacobite, who died in his 80s. The latter's eldest son, Lt.Colonel Charles [1725-1746], who commanded the Frasers of Lovat at Culloden, was murdered on the orders of the Duke of Cumberland. His third son, Captain Simon [1732-1759] was killed while serving with the 78th Fraser Highlanders at Quebec in 1759. When the second and only surving son, William [1730-1792] died unmarried, the estates were split between his two sisters, Martha [1727-1803], who married Colin Mackenzie, 6th of Kilcoy, and Elyza Fraser [1734-1814], eventually passing out of the family.

In 1956 Inverallochy was bequeathed to the RC Diocese of Aberdeen, and in 1976 Castle Fraser was placed in the care of the National Trust for Scotland. The Castle, which has been faithfully restored, is one of the Trust's most popular tourist attractions, and is open daily from April to October, with the grounds and garden being open all year.

Castle Fraser

2

Cairnbulg Castle

History

Cairnbulg Castle is of interest for three reasons. It is one of the oldest buildings in Aberdeenshire still to be inhabited by the family who built it, whose home it is. It is of great interest to students of mediaeval Castles and architecture, for there are many gaps in our knowledge of its history, and thus much scope for study and speculation. Finally, it contains a collection of family portraits which is rare in Scotland, not because most of them are by painters of any distinction, for they are not, but because there is a portrait of every Laird since 1570, and in many cases of their wives, brothers, sisters or in-laws, and this is very unusual.

In the years before 1308-9, the Comyns, Earls of Buchan, held all the land in this part of Aberdeenshire which is still known as Buchan. Before the defeat of the Norse at the Battle of Largs in 1263 and the death of King Haakon in the following year, the .coast of Buchan was exposed to their invasions. The Earls of Buchan were responsible for coastal defence and built a number of Castles round the coast of which the first stone Castle here was probably one. Although the site does not nowadays appear to be near enough to the coast to be much use for coastal defence, there are strong reasons for supposing that at the time it was built, it was actually right on the estuary of the Water of Philorth, and its old name, Philorth, actually means *Pool of the River Orth*.

The site may not have been dissimilar to that of Red Castle at Lunan Bay, just south of Montrose.

On this particular stretch of coast, the sea has been receding over the last few hundred years. The soils, levels, stones, etc., in the fields on the seaward side of the Castle mound show every sign of having been the bed of a tidal river, if not the sea shore itself. An old print shows a ship beached on the shore and boats drawn up along it, not far from the foot of the mound. The sand dunes between Fraserburgh and Cairnbulg Point probably only grew up during the nineteenth and twentieth centuries.

The author remembers that in her childhood there was a large expanse of flat sand with no dunes at all from a point opposite Philorth Bridge right to the present mouth of the river, and the river itself was still changing course. It only settled finally in its present course in the late 1930s, and the dunes opposite the Castle have grown up since 1940. Until then it was possible to see the sea from ground floor level.

In the Wars of Independence, the Comyns sided with the English against Robert I [the Bruce], and after he had defeated them at the Battle of Barra Hill [Inverurie] in the winter of 1308-9, he carried out an operation known as the *Harrying of the Buchan*, in which he destroyed all the Castles of the Earldom, so that they could never again be held against him, and he forfeited the Earldom and divided it up among various of his supporters. The Earl of Ross, who had eventually joined Bruce, received this part of Buchan and the ruins of the first Castle.

In 1375 the daughter and co-heiress of the 5th Earl of Ross, Joanna, married Sir Alexander Fraser of Cowie, whose grandfather had been Sir Alexander Fraser [Bruce's Chamberlain], who had married Bruce's sister Mary, widow of Sir Neil Campbell of Lochow [Lochawe]. The Ross lands in Buchan were Joanna's tocher [English: dowry], and probably circa 1380 they restored the Castle.

At least the upper floors of the main tower appear to date from that time, although the ground floor may have been rebuilt earlier or never actually destroyed, since the masonry is quite different from that of the upper floors, although probably also dating from the fourteenth century. Either then or later were added a courtyard and outbuildings to the east of the tower, where there are still foundations of buildings underground. [Note the foundations of the tower which are just huge stones placed on the clay mound which forms the site, and which can be seen outside.]

At some stage, possibly in the sixteenth century, the staircase tower was added and a wing running east from it, and probably later still, possibly at the time of the *War of the Rough Wooing* when Henry VIII tried to marry his son Edward to the young Mary Queen of Scots in 1545, the round tower was built and also the part of the Castle now comprising the front hall and the room above it. The exact dates when any part of the Castle was built are a matter of speculation. What we do know from the masonry and various pictures of it when a ruin, is that it has been altered a number of times. At the foot of the round tower the old gun loops are still to be seen, one designed to fire north along the east face of the courtyard wall, covering the entrance gateway which was at the north-east corner of the east wall of the court-yard; one to fire south-east where the only dry ground was; and one to fire west along the south face of the range between the two towers, which was narrower than the present house; and one at the first floor level above the latter.

The family continued here at the Castle, the old Manor Place of Philorth, until the late sixteenth century. In the last quarter of that century, Sir Alexander Fraser, 8th of Philorth, built the town of Fraserburgh, improved the Harbour and founded a University there and built another

Castle to which he moved [which was until recently the Kinnaird Head Lighthouse]. As a result, he got heavily into debt and in 1613 was obliged to sell this Castle and a great deal of land.

The Castle was sold to Alexander Fraser of Durris, on condition that should he or his descendants ever wish to sell it, they would first offer it to Sir Alexander or his descendants. The agreement was not honoured and the Castle passed from one family to another. From 1613 to 1631 or 1637 it belonged to Fraser of Durris, then until 1703 to Fraser of Muchalls [created Lord Fraser], then from 1703 to 1739 to Thomas Buchan of Auchmacoy and his son, then until 1775 to Alexander Aberdein and his son.

From 1775 to 1801 it belonged to George, 3rd Earl of Aberdeen, who vandalised it to build and improve other houses in the district in which he kept his mistresses. By 1780 both towers were in a ruinous condition, and the building in between a ruin. After him it belonged to his illegitimate son John Gordon until 1863, when the ruin was bought by Mr. Duthie of the Aberdeen shipbuilding firm who built and owned the famous tea clippers. In 1896 his nephew, Sir John Duthie, restored the Castle using granite, which was his wife's tocher from her father who was a stone merchant. Their initials and motto are over the present front door. He died in 1923 and in 1934 the late Lord Saltoun, 11th in descent from the 8th Laird, bought it back and modernised it.

Since 1966 it has belonged to the author, who did further modernisation then. In 1989-90 extensive repairs were done and both towers, the staircase tower and the west face were re-harled.

The Castle is open to the public BY APPOINTMENT ONLY.

Cairnbulg Castle

Fraserburgh

Harbour, 1993

Fraserburgh Castle [above], built in 1570 by Sir Alexander Fraser, 8th laird of Philorth. A powerful lantern was added to the top floor in 1787, when it became the Northern Lighthouse Board's first lighthouse and a lightkeeper was hired. The 19th Lord Saltoun served as Convenor of the Scottish Lifeboat Council for more than 20 years. A fitting monument to Scotland's lighthouse service, the old castle at Kinnaird Head is now a museum, owned by Historic Scotland and operated by Scotland's Museum Trust. Open to the public from April 1st to the end of September, the crowning glory of any visit to the museum is a unique guided tour to the very top of the lighthouse - just 75 yards and 72 steps from the museum. To the left is the old Wine Tower.

[See next page for Mrs. James Cardno's 1850 drawing of the Keep of Fraserburgh Castle, Wine Tower and Ancient Pigeon House.]

The Legend of the Wine Tower

The Wine Tower is an old three storey quadrangular building standing on top of a cave, rising from a rock which overhangs the sea, about fifty yards east of Fraserburgh Castle. Although no history of the structure exists, there is a legend, related in verse form, which deals with the tragic tale of two young lovers. The maiden's father, who wanted her to marry a rich old man, arranged for the young man to be tied up in the cave under the tower, and left to die. When he later presented the body to his daughter, she clutched her lover's corpse and threw herself into the sea.

1 2 3

(1) Keep of Fraserburgh Castle (made the Light House)

(2) The Wine Tower (part of the old Fort)

(3) Ancient Pigeon House (since removed)

The story of the wine tower is purely apocryphal. The 6th laird bought Faithlie from Sir Henry Mercer of Aldie in 1504. It might have been his or the 7th laird's daughter who was involved. The 8th, 9th and 10th lairds all seem to have been such gentle, kindly creatures that one cannot envisage them doing such a thing. But if the young man was a 'baddie' bent on atouching an innocent and very young girl, they might well have popped him in the dungeon for the night, without any real intention of drowning him, and desperate to protect their daughter.

I think the wine tower was part of a fort which was there long before the 8th laird built his castle, and I see no reason why the girl should have been a Fraser at all - she may have been a Mercer!

The Ballad of the Wine Tower

from *Pratt's Buchan* written circa 140 years ago

Love wove a chaplet passing fair,
Within Kinnaird's proud Tower ;
Where joyous youth, and beauty rare,
Lay captive to his power.

But woe is me ! - alack the day !
Pride spurned the simple wreath ;
And scattering all those blooms away,
He doomed sweet love to death.

No bridal wreath, O maiden fair !
Thy brow shall e'er adorn ;
A father's stern behest is there,
Of pride and avarice born.

What boots to him thy vows, thy tears ?
What boots thy plighted troth ?
One, rich in pelf, and hoar in years,
Is deemed of seemlier worth.

Than he who, with but love to guide,
Keeps tryst in yonder bower ;
Where ruffians - hired by ruffian pride,-
His stalwart limbs secure.

Where rolls old ocean's surging tide,
The *Wine Tower* beetling stands,
Right o'er a cavern deep and wide -
No work of mortal hands.

Dark as the dark expanse of hell,
That cavern's dreary space ;
Whence never captive came to tell
The secrets of the place.

There, bound in cruel fetters, lies
The lover fond and true ;
No more to glad the maiden's eyes,
No more to bless her view !

No pitying hand relieves his want,
No loving eye his woe ;
A hapless prey to hunger gaunt,-
He dies in torments slow !

Thus slept the youth in death's embrace :-
Darkly the tyrant smiled ;
The corpse then dragged from that dread place,
And bore it to his child.

Ay, say, he cried, *what greets thy view* ?
Can'st trace these wholesome charms ?
Henceforth a fitter mate shall woo
And win thee to his arms.

Didst think that these, my brave broad lands,
His love would well repay ?
No, minion, no ! - for other hands
Shall bear the prize away.

These direful words the maid arrest,-
A marble hue she bore ;
Then sinking on that clay-cold breast,
We part, she cried, *no more.*

No more shall man his will oppose,
Nor man the wrong abet ;
Our virgin love in fealty rose,
In fealty it shall set.

Then clasping close that shrouded form,
Which erst her love inspired ;
Fearless she breasted cliff and storm,
By love and frenzy fired.

Farewell, O ruthless sire, she cried,
Farewell earth's all of good ;
Our bridal waits below the tide,-
Then plunged beneath the flood !

Sketch from *The Frasers of Philorth*

CAIRNBULG CASTLE

THE OLD MANOR HOUSE OF PHILORTH

Sir Alexander Fraser
8th Laird of Philorth
[c.1536-1623]
Founder of Fraserburgh

by an unknown artist

ALEX^R FRASER
LAIRD OF PHILORTH
JAMIESON

Alexander Fraser
9th Laird of Philorth
[c.1570-1636]
m. Margaret, dau. of
George Abernethy
7th Lord Saltoun

by George Jamieson, 1625

ALEX.R FRASER
LORD SALTOUN
1670
BY SCOUGAL

Alexander Fraser
10th Laird of Philorth
[1604-1693]
10th Lord Saltoun
(inherited title from mother
in 1669)

by David Scougal

ALEX.R FRASER
MASTER OF SALTOUN
1670
BY SCOUGAL

Alexander Fraser
Master of Saltoun
[1630-1682]

by David Scougal

WILLIAM FRASER
LORD SALTOUN

William Fraser
11th Lord Saltoun
[1654-1714/5

by the Lanark Painter

Margaret Sharp
[1664-1734]
dau. & co-heiress of
Archbishop of St. Andrew's

by an unknown artist

ALEXR FRASER
LORD SALTOUN
1714

Alexander Fraser
12th Lord Saltoun
[1685-1748]

by Sir Godfrey Kneller

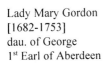

Lady Mary Gordon
[1682-1753]
dau. of George
1st Earl of Aberdeen

by an unknown artist, 1707

Alexander Fraser
13th Lord Saltoun
[1710-1751]

by Joseph Highmore

GEORGE FRASER
LORD SALTOUN
1751
BY MARTIN

George Fraser
14th Lord Saltoun
[1720-1781]

attributed to David Martin

Alexander Fraser
15th Lord Saltoun
[1758-1793]

by Samuel West

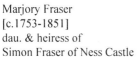

Marjory Fraser
[c.1753-1851]
dau. & heiress of
Simon Fraser of Ness Castle

by Lady Gordon Cumming

Lt-Gen Alexander George Fraser
16th Lord Saltoun
[1785-1853]
Waterloo Saltoun

by James Lonsdale

Alexander George Fraser
16th Lord Saltoun
Uniform of the First Guards
Waterloo Portrait

by Lawrence

Alexander Fraser
17th Lord Saltoun
[1820-1886]
Big Zander

by Alexander Blaikie, 1859

Charlotte Evans
[c.1825-1890]
dau. of Thomas Browne Evans
and Charlotte Simeon

by Samuel West, 1849

Alexander William Fraser
18th Lord Saltoun
[1851-1933]
Uniform of the Gordon Highlanders

by Edwin Ward, 1898

Alexander Arthur Fraser
19th Lord Saltoun
[1886-1979]

circa 1966

Alexander Fraser
Master of Saltoun
[1921-1944]
Photo used for portrait

Alexander Arthur Fraser
19th Lord Saltoun
Photo used for portrait

circa 1950

Dorothy Welby
[1890-1985]
dau. of Sir Charles Welby
and Lady Maria Hervey

by Bertram Parks, 1920

Wedding of Lady Saltoun and Captain Ramsay
6th October 1956 - Fraserburgh

Back Row:	LCol David Fraser (now General Sir David, bride's cousin & chief usher), Admiral the Hon Sir Alexander Ramsay (bridegroom's father), Col Peter Thorne (best man), the Hon Elizabeth Ormsby-Gore (bride's best friend), Lord Saltoun (bride's father), the Hon Mrs Wardlaw Ramsay (bride's aunt, her father's sister).
Front Row:	Lady Patricia Ramsay (bridegroom's mother), Queen Ingrid of Denmark, Queen Elizabeth The Queen Mother, Lady Saltoun (bride's mother).

3

Lines of Succession

The Early Frasers

To illustrate the complex relationship of the Early Frasers and the lines of succession of the Frasers of Philorth (Lords Saltoun) and the Highland branch of the Frasers of Lovat (Lords Lovat), I have included Charts prepared by Marie Fraser from Tables made by my cousin, General Sir David Fraser, grandson of 18th Lord Saltoun. His comments are worth noting:

References to the Frasers and their connections are found in most public archives in Scotland as well as in collections such as the Spalding Club's *Antiquities of Aberdeenshire* and other works. Then there are the particular books and histories specifically about the family, such as Alexander Mackenzie's *History of the Frasers of Lovat*, Lord Saltoun's *The Frasers of Philorth*, and - very specifically - Duncan Warrand's *Some Fraser Pedigrees*, with the latter author's extensive coverage of Parish records in Inverness-shire. There are also, of course, standard works of reference such as Burke's *Peerage* and *Landed Gentry*; and last, but not least, the *Wardlaw MS* whose author, Rev. James Fraser of Phopachy, has been regarded as fanciful in his account of the earlier origins of the Fraser name, but who was probably very well-informed on his own immediate times in the seventeenth century.

Early Frasers' Armorial Seals, Woodcuts of -

No. 1

No. 2

No. 4

No. 3

No. 5

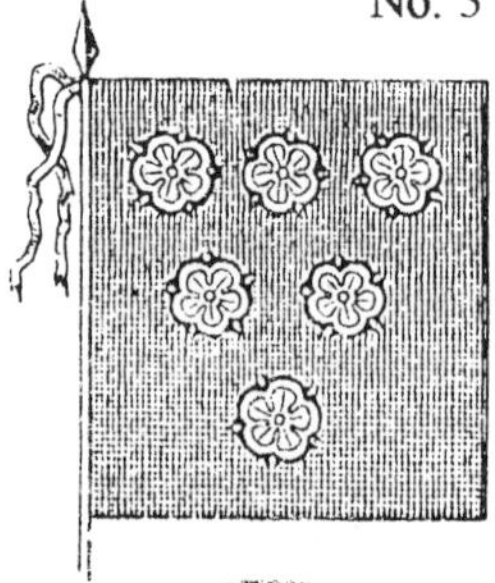

No. 7

No. 6

No. 8

No. 9

1) Richard Fraser, *ante* 1276.
2) Sir Richard Fraser, 1297.
3) Sir Andrew Fraser, 1297.
4) William Fraser, Bishop of St. Andrew's, 1279-97. Seal as Metropolitan.
5) William Fraser, Bishop of St. Andrew's 1279-97. Episcopal Seal.
6) Sir Simon Fraser (Filius), 1297.
7) Banner of Sir Simon Fraser (Filius), 1300.
8) William Fraser, 1296.
9) Hugh Fraser, 1st of Lovat, 1377 & *c.*1390.
10) Declaration of Arbroath, 1320, signed by Sir Alexander Fraser, Chamberlain of Scotland, 1319-26.

No. 10

Declaration of Arbroath
Letter to Pope John XXII - 6th April 1320

But if our King were to abandon the cause by being ready to make us, or our kingdom, subject to the King of England or to the English, we should at once do our utmost to expel him as our enemy and the betrayer of his own rights and ours, and should choose some other man to be our king, who would be ready to defend us. For so long as a hundred of us shall remain alive, we are resolved never to submit to the domination of the English. It is not for glory, wealth or honour that we are fighting, but for freedom and freedom only, which no true man ever surrenders except with his life."

1st Generation:	Simon Fraser [Keith], Gilbert Fraser & Bernard Fraser
2nd Generation:	Oliver Fraser, Udard Fraser & Thomas Fraser

Issue of:

Udard Fraser :	Sir Bernard Fraser, Sir Gilbert Fraser & Adam Fraser
Sir Gilbert Fraser :	John, Sir Simon, Sir Andrew & William [Bishop]
John Fraser :	Sir Richard Fraser & Sir Alexander Fraser of Cornton
Sir Simon Fraser :	Sir Simon (d.1291): - Sir Simon (d.1306) - 2 daughters
Sir Richard Fraser :	Sir Andrew Fraser (d.1297)
Sir Andrew Fraser :	*Sir Alexander*, ancestor of the Frasers of Philorth, *Sir Simon*, ancestor of the Frasers of Lovat, Sir Andrew & *Sir James* Fraser of Frendraught, whose line ended with his great granddaughter Mauld Fraser.

Frasers of Philorth [Lords Saltoun]

The Abernethy Line

	Lords of Parliament	Birth	Death
Malcolm III, King of Scots [1058-1093] m. 2ndly St. Margaret			
Eth or Ethelred, 1st Earl of Fife, last Abbot of Dunkeld			c.1128
Duff [possibly predeceased his Father]			
Gillemichael, 3rd Earl of Fife			c.1133 or 1139
Hugh, Lay Abbott of Abernethy			ante 1164
Orm de Abernethy, Lay Abbott			before 1190
Laurence de Abernethy, last Lay Abbott			c.1245
Patrick de Abernethy			c.1254
Sir William Abernethy, 1st of Saltoun			c.1296
Sir William Abernethy, 2nd of Saltoun			ante 1330
Sir William Abernethy, 3rd of Saltoun			ante 1350
Sir George Abernethy, 4th of Saltoun			ante 1371
Sir George Abernethy, 5th of Saltoun			ante 1400
Sir William Abernethy, 6th of Saltoun			1420
William Abernethy, 7th of Saltoun			1411 k.
Sir Laurence Abernethy, 8th of Saltoun	1st Lord Saltoun		1460
William Abernethy	2nd Lord Saltoun		1488 s.p.
James Abernethy	3rd Lord Saltoun		1504/5
Alexander Abernethy	4th Lord Saltoun		1527
William Abernethy	5th Lord Saltoun		1543
Alexander Abernethy	6th Lord Saltoun	1537	1587
George Abernethy	7th Lord Saltoun		1590 s.p.
John Abernethy	8th Lord Saltoun		1617
Alexander Abernethy	9th Lord Saltoun	1611	1668 s.p.

Frasers of Philorth [Lords Saltoun]

The Philorth Line
[Chiefs of Clan Fraser]

	Lords of Parliament	Birth	Death
Sir Alexander Fraser, 1st of Cowie [Chamberlain of Scotland 1319-26]			1332 k.
Sir William Fraser, 2nd of Cowie		c.1319	1346 k.
Sir Alexander Fraser 3rd of Cowie & Durris, 1st of Philorth		c.1345	1410
Sir William Fraser, 2nd of Philorth		c.1377	1442
Sir Alexander Fraser, 3rd of Philorth		c.1410	1482
Alexander Fraser, 4th of Philorth		c.1432	1486
Alexander Fraser, 5th of Philorth		c.1472	1500 s.p.
Sir William Fraser, 6th of Philorth		c.1474	1513 k.
Alexander Fraser, 7th of Philorth		c.1495	1569
Sir Alexander Fraser, 8th of Philorth		c.1536	1623
Alexander Fraser, 9th of Philorth		c.1570	1636
Alexander Fraser, 10th of Philorth	10th Lord Saltoun	1604	1693
William Fraser, 11th of Philorth	11th Lord Saltoun	1654	1714/5
Alexander Fraser, 12th of Philorth	12th Lord Saltoun	1685	1748
Alexander Fraser, 13th of Philorth	13th Lord Saltoun	1710	1751 s.p.
George Fraser, 14th of Philorth	14th Lord Saltoun	1720	1781
Alexander Fraser, 15th of Philorth	15th Lord Saltoun	1758	1793
Alexander Fraser, 16th of Philorth	16th Lord Saltoun	1785	1853 s.p.
Alexander Fraser, 17th of Philorth	17th Lord Saltoun	1820	1886
Alexander Fraser, 18th of Philorth	18th Lord Saltoun	1851	1933
Alexander Arthur, 19th of Philorth	19th Lord Saltoun	1886	1979
Flora Marjory Fraser, 20th of Philorth	20th Lady Saltoun	1930	

Flora Marjory Fraser, The Lady Saltoun

1 Flora Marjory Fraser, 20th Lady Saltoun (b. 1930)
2 Alexander Fraser, 19th Lord Saltoun (1886-1979)
3 Dorothy Welby, m. 1920
4 Alexander Fraser, 18th Lord Saltoun (1851-1933)
5 Mary Helena Gratton-Bellew, m. 1885
6 Sir Charles Welby (1865-1938)
7 Lady Maria Hervey, m. 1887
8 Alexander Fraser, 17th Lord Saltoun (1820-1886)
9 Charlotte Evans, m. 1849
10 Thomas Arthur Grattan-Bellew (1820-1863)
11 Pauline Grattan, m. 1858
12 Sir William Welby (1829-1898)
13 Victoria Stuart-Wortley, m. 1863
14 Lord Augustus Hervey (1837-1875)
15 Marianna Hodnett, m. 1861
16 William Fraser of Philorth (1791-1845)
17 Elizabeth Macdowell Grant of Arndilly, m. 1818
32 Alexander Fraser, 15th Lord Saltoun (1758-1793)
33 Marjory Fraser of Ness Castle, m. 1784
64 George Fraser, 14th Lord Saltoun (1720-1781)
65 Eleanor Gordon of Kinellar, c. 1755
128 Alexander Fraser, 12th Lord Saltoun (1685-1748)
129 Lady Mary Gordon, m. 1707
256 William Fraser, 11th Lord Saltoun (1654-1714/5)
257 Margaret Sharp, m. 1683
512 Alexander Fraser of Philorth (1630-1682)
513 Lady Anne Kerr, m. 1651/2
1,024 Alexander Fraser, 10th Lord Saltoun (1604-1693)
1,025 Elizabeth Seton of Meldrum, m. 1630
2,048 Alexander Fraser, 9th of Philorth (c.1570-1636)
2,049 Margaret Abernethy, m. 1595

Note:
An Ahnentafel records a person's ancestry (eg. counting backwards, each generation is doubled - 2 parents, 4 grandparents, 8 great grandparents, etc.).

Flora Marjory Fraser, The Lady Saltoun (Cont'd.)

4,096 Alexander Fraser, 8th of Philorth (c.1536-1623)
4,097 Magdalen Ogilvie of Dunlugus, m. 1559
8,192 Alexander Fraser of Philorth (c.1518-1564)
8,193 Lady Beatrice Keith, m. c.1535
16,384 Alexander Fraser, 7th of Philorth (c.1495-1569)
16,385 Katherine Menzies of Pitfodels, m. 1516
32,768 Sir William Fraser, 6th of Philorth (c.1474-1513 k)
32,769 Elizabeth Keith of Inverugie, m. c.1494
65,536 Alexander Fraser, 4th of Philorth (c.1432-1486)
65,537 Lady Margaret Hay, m. c.1470
131,072 Sir Alexander Fraser, 3rd of Philorth (c.1410-1482)
131,073 Marjorie Menzies of Findon, m. c.1430
262,144 Sir William Fraser, 2nd of Philorth (c.1377-1442)
262,145 Elinor Douglas, b. ca 1385, m. c.1404
524,288 Sir Alexander Fraser 3rd of Cowie & Durris, 1st of Philorth (c.1345-1410)
524,289 Lady Joanna Ross, m. 1375
1,048,576 Sir William Fraser, 2nd of Cowie (c.1319-1346 k)
1,048,577 Margaret Moray of Bothwell, m. c.1342
2,097,152 Sir Alexander Fraser, 1st of Cowie (k.1332)
2,097,153 Lady Mary Bruce, m. 1316 *[sister of Robert the Bruce]*
4,194,304 Sir Andrew Fraser, 3rd Touch-Fraser, d. 1297 *[also father of Sir Simon Fraser*
4,194,305 Spouse of Sir Andrew Fraser *- Lovat Line]*
8,388,608 Sir Richard Fraser, 2nd of Touch-Fraser
8,388,609 Spouse of Sir Richard Fraser
16,777,216 John Fraser of Oliver Castle, d. c.1263
16,777,217 Alicia Cunigberg
33,554,432 Sir Gilbert Fraser, 1st of Oliver Castle
33,554,433 Christian ? Lascelles
67,108,864 Udard Fraser in East Lothian *[alive in 1200]*
67,108,865 Spouse of Udard Fraser

This Ahnentafel traces Lady Saltoun's ancestry over 25 generations.

Frasers of Lovat [Lords Lovat]

	Lords of Parliament	Birth	Death
The Lovat Line			
[Chiefs of Clan Fraser of Lovat]			
Sir Simon Fraser, 1st MacShimi			1333 k.
Sir Alexander Fraser, 2nd MacShimi			1361
Hugh Fraser, 3rd MacShimi, 1st of Lovat			1410
Alexander Fraser, 4th MacShimi, 2nd of Lovat			1415/6
Alexander Fraser, 5th MacShimi, 3rd of Lovat		c.1375	1436 s.p.
Hugh Fraser, 6th MacShimi, 4th of Lovat		1377	1440
Thomas Fraser, 7th MacShimi, 5th of Lovat		c.1417	c.1455
Hugh Fraser, 8th MacShimi, 6th of Lovat	1st Lord Lovat	c.1436	1501
Thomas Fraser, 9th MacShimi	2nd Lord Lovat	1460	1524
Hugh Fraser, 10th MacShimi	3rd Lord Lovat	1494	1544 k.
Alexander Fraser, 11th MacShimi	4th Lord Lovat	1527	1557
Hugh Fraser, 12th MacShimi	5th Lord Lovat	1547	1575/6
Simon Fraser, 13th MacShimi	6th Lord Lovat	1570	1633
Hugh Fraser, 14th MacShimi	7th Lord Lovat	1591	1645
Hugh Fraser, 15th MacShimi	8th Lord Lovat	1642/3	1672
Hugh Fraser, 16th MacShimi	9th Lord Lovat	1666	1696 s.p.
Thomas Fraser,17th MacShimi	10th Lord Lovat	1631	1699
Simon Fraser, 18th MacShimi	11th Lord Lovat	1668	1747

[Simon Fraser, 11th Lord Lovat was executed 9th April 1747 for his role in the Jacobite Rebellion and the Lovat title was attained by an Act of Parliament]

Frasers of Lovat [Lords Lovat]

The Lovat Line
[Chiefs of Clan Fraser of Lovat]

	Lords of Parliament	Birth	Death
Simon Fraser, 19th MacShimi		1726	1782 s.p.
Archibald Fraser, 20th MacShimi		1736	1815 s.p.

[After the death of Archibald Fraser, 20th MacShimi, on 8th December 1815, the chiefship of the Frasers of Lovat passed to the Strichen line via the 2nd son of Alexander Fraser, 4th Lord Lovat; when Thomas Alexander Fraser, 10th of Strichen was created Baron Lovat in Peerage of the United Kingdom in 1837, and the attainder was reversed in his favour by an Act of Parliament in 1857, reviving the original Scots Peerage]

Thomas Fraser, 21st MacShimi	14th Lord Lovat	1802	1875
Simon Fraser, 22nd MacShimi	15th Lord Lovat	1828	1887
Simon Fraser, 23rd MacShimi	16th Lord Lovat	1871	1933
Simon Fraser, 24th MacShimi	17th Lord Lovat	1911	1995
Simon Fraser, 25th MacShimi	18th Lord Lovat	1977	

[The 25th MacShimi and 18th Lord Lovat, Chief of Clan Fraser of Lovat, is the grandson of 17th Lord Lovat]

Simon Fraser, 18th Lord Lovat | *Simon Fraser, 11th Lord Lovat*

1 Simon Fraser, 18th Lord Lovat (b. 1977)

2 Simon Fraser, Master of Lovat (1939-1994)
3 Virginia Grose, m. 1972
4 Simon Fraser, 17th Lord Lovat (1911-1995)
5 Rosamund Broughton, m. 1938
8 Simon Fraser, 16th Lord Lovat (1871-1933)
9 Laura Lister, m. 1910
16 Simon Fraser, 15th Lord Lovat (1828-1887)
17 Alice Mary Weld Blundell, m. 1866
32 Thomas Fraser, 14th Lord Lovat (1802-1875)
33 Charlotte Jerningham, m. 1823
64 Capt Alexander Fraser, 9th Strichen (1765-1803)
65 Amelia Leslie of Balquhain, m. 1800
128 Alexander Fraser, 8th Strichen (c.1733-1794)
129 Jean Menzies, m. 1764
256 Alexander Fraser, 7th Strichen (c.1699-1775)
257 Lady Ann Campbell, Countess of Bute, m. 1731

512 Alexander Fraser, 5th Strichen (c.1659-1699)
513 Amelia Stewart, m. 1697
1,024 Thomas Fraser, 4th Strichen (c.1630-1685)
1,025 Marion Irvine of Fedderat, m. 1656
2,048 Thomas Fraser, 3rd Strichen (1612-1656)
2,049 Christian Forbes of Pitsligo, m. 1628
4,096 Thomas Fraser, 2nd Strichen (d. Mar 1644/5)
4,097 Christian Forbes of Tolquhoun, m. 1606
8,192 Thomas Fraser, Knockie & Strichen (1548-1612)
8,193 Isobel Forbes of Corsindae, m. c.1580
16,384 Alexander Fraser, 4th Lord Lovat (1527-57)
16,385 Janet Campbell of Cawdor, m. c.1546

1 Simon Fraser, 11th Lord Lovat (1668-1747)

2 Thomas Fraser, 10th Lord Lovat (1631-99)
3 Sybilla Macleod of Macleod, m. 1665
4 Hugh Fraser, 7th Lord Lovat (1591-1645)
5 Isobel Wemyss of Wemyss, m. 1614
8 Simon Fraser, 6th Lord Lovat (1570-1633)
9 Catherine Mackenzie of Kintail, m. 1589
16 Hugh Fraser, 5th Lord Lovat (1547-75/6)
17 Lady Elizabeth Stewart, m. 1565
32 Alexander Fraser, 4th Lord Lovat (1527-57)
33 Janet Campbell of Cawdor, m. c.1546

Note:
The Ahnentafel of the 18th Lord Lovat compares his ancestry with that of the 11th Lord Lovat. They share the same ancestry from the 4th Lord Lovat.

Simon Fraser, 18th Lord Lovat
(Cont'd.)

8,388,608 Sir Simon Fraser, k. 1333
8,388,609 Spouse of Sir Simon Fraser
16,777,216 Sir Andrew Fraser, 3rd Touch-Fraser
16,777,217 Spouse of Sir Andrew Fraser
33,554,432 Sir Richard Fraser, 2nd Touch-Fraser
33,554,433 Spouse of Sir Richard Fraser
67,108,864 John Fraser of Oliver Castle, d.c.1263
67,108,865 Alicia de Cunigberg
134,217,728 Sir Gilbert Fraser, 1st Oliver Castle
134,217,729 Christian ? Lascelles
268,435,456 Udard Fraser in East Lothian
268,435,457 Spouse of Udard Fraser

Lord Lovat [above left] opens Shinty Game

Simon Fraser, 11th Lord Lovat
(Cont'd.)

64 Hugh Fraser, 3rd Lord Lovat (1494-1544)
65 Janet Ross of Balnagowan, m. c.1526
128 Thomas Fraser, 2nd Lord Lovat (1460-1524)
129 Janet Gordon of Auchindoun, m. 1493
256 Hugh Fraser, 1st Lord Lovat (1436-1501)
257 Margaret Lyon, m. c.1459
512 Thomas Fraser, 5th Lovat (c.1417-1455)
513 Lady Janet Dunbar, m. 1433
1,024 Hugh Fraser, 4th Lovat (1377-1440)
1,025 Janet Fenton of Beaufort, m. 1416
2,048 Alexander Fraser, 2nd Lovat, d.c.1416
2,049 Elizabeth Keith
4,096 Hugh Fraser, 1st Lovat, d. 1410
4,097 Isobel Wemyss of Wemyss
8,192 Sir Alexander Fraser of Brotherton
8,193 Miss Moray of Bothwell
16,384 Sir Simon Fraser, k. 1333
16,385 Lady Margaret Sinclair
32,768 Sir Andrew Fraser, 3rd Touch-Fraser
32,769 Spouse of Sir Andrew Fraser
65,536 Sir Richard Fraser, 2nd Touch-Fraser
65,537 Spouse of Sir Richard Fraser
131,072 John Fraser of Oliver Castle, d.c.1263
131,073 Alicia de Cunigberg
262,144 Sir Gilbert Fraser, 1st Oliver Castle
262,145 Christian ? Lascelles
524,288 Udard Fraser in East Lothian
524,289 Spouse of Udard Fraser

Frasers of Muchalls [Lords Fraser]

	Lords of Parliament	Birth	Death
Sir Alexander Fraser, 1st of Cornton			1306
Frasers of Cornton *[2 or 3 Generations]*			
Thomas Fraser of Cornton, 1st of Kinmundy			c.1392
Thomas Fraser of Cornton, 2nd of Kinmundy			c.1427
Thomas Fraser of Stoneywood & Muchalls *[Castle Fraser]*			c.1475
Sir Andrew Fraser, 2nd of Muchalls			1505
Thomas Fraser, 3rd of Muchalls			1535
Andrew Fraser, 4th of Muchalls			1549
Andrew Fraser, 5th of Muchalls			ante 1563
Michael Fraser, 6th of Muchalls		1544	ante1588/9
Andrew Fraser, 7th of Muchalls	1st Lord Fraser	1574	1636
Andrew Fraser	2nd Lord Fraser	c.1595	1656-8
Andrew Fraser	3rd Lord Fraser	c.1635	1674
Charles Fraser	4th Lord Fraser	c.1662	1716 s.p.

The Inverallochy / Castle Fraser Line

	Birth	Death
Sir Simon Fraser, 1st of Inverallochy	1597	1620
Simon Fraser, 2nd of Inverallochy	c.1618	1659
Simon Fraser, 3rd of Inverallochy	c.1648	1683
Alexander Fraser, 4th of Inverallochy	c.1670	1698 s.p.
William Fraser, 5th of Inverallochy	c.1672	1716/7
Charles Fraser, 6th of Inverallochy *[Auld Inverallochy]*	c.1705	1787
Martha Fraser, 7th of Inverallochy m. Colin Mackenzie, 6th of Kilcoy	1727	1803

	Birth	Death
The Inverallochy / Castle Fraser Line		
Lieut-Gen Alexander Mackenzie-Fraser	1758	1809
Col Charles Mackenzie-Fraser	1792	1871
Col Frederick Mackenzie-Fraser	1831	1897

Colonel Charles Mackenzie-Fraser
[1792-1871]
by B.R. Faulkner

Jane Hay Mackenzie-Fraser
[1799-1861]
after Sir Thomas Lawrence

Frederick Mackenzie-Fraser

1 Frederick Mackenzie-Fraser (1831-1897 s.p.)
2 Charles Mackenzie-Fraser (1792-1871)
3 Jane Hay of Haystown, m. 1817
4 Alexander Mackenzie-Fraser (1756-1809)
5 Helen Mackenzie, m. 1786
8 Colin Mackenzie, 6th Kilcoy
9 Martha Fraser, 7th Inverallochy, m. 1747
18 Charles Fraser, 6th Inverallochy (c.1705-1787)
19 Anne Udney of Udney
36 William Fraser, 5th Inverallochy (c.1672-1716/7)
37 Lady Elizabeth Erskine
72 Simon Fraser, 3rd Inverallochy (c.1648-83)
73 Lady Marjory [Margaret] Erskine, m. 1669 m. 2nd

144 Simon Fraser, 2nd Inverallochy (c.1618-1659)
145 Elizabeth Muray of Claremount, m. c.1645

288 Sir Simon Fraser, 1st Inverallochy (1597-1620)
289 Jean Moncrieff of Moncrieff, m. 1616

576 Simon Fraser, 6th Lord Lovat (1570-1633)
577 Jean Stewart, m. 1595/6

1,152 Hugh Fraser, 5th Lord Lovat (1547-1575/6)
1,153 Lady Elizabeth Stewart, m. 1565

Charles Fraser, 4th Lord Fraser

Castle Fraser from the north, by C.J. Hullmande

1 Charles Fraser, 4th Lord Fraser (c.1662-1716)s.

2 Andrew Fraser, 3rd Lord Fraser (c.1635-1674)
3 Katherine Fraser of Lovat, m. 1658
4 Andrew Fraser, 2nd Lord Fraser (c.1595-1656)
5 Anne Haldane of Gleneagles, m. 1634
6 Hugh Fraser, 7th Lord Lovat (1591-1645)
7 Isobel Wemyss of Wemyss, m. 1614
8 Andrew Fraser, 1st Lord Fraser (1574-1636)
9 Lady Elizabeth Douglas, m. 1592
12 Simon Fraser, 6th Lord Lovat (1570-1633)
13 Catherine Mackenzie of Kintail, m. 1589
16 Michael Fraser, 6th Muchalls (1544-1588)
17 Isobel Forbes of Monymusk, m. c.1571
24 Hugh Fraser, 5th Lord Lovat (1547-1575/6)
25 Lady Elizabeth Stewart, m. 1565

Note:
The Ahnentafel of Frederick Mackenzie-Fraser compares his ancestry with that of the 4th Lord Fraser of Muchalls. They shared the same ancestry from the 6th Lord Lovat. Frederick Mackenzie-Fraser's Ahnentafel traces his ancestry through the Frasers of Inverallochy.

Frederick Mackenzie-Fraser
(Cont'd.)

2,304 Alexander Fraser, 4th Lord Lovat (1527-1557)
2,305 Janet Campbell of Cawdor, m. c.1546

4,608 Hugh Fraser, 3rd Lord Lovat (c.1494-1544)
4,609 Janet Ross of Balnagowan, m. c.1526

9,216 Thomas Fraser, 2nd Lord Lovat (1460-1524)
9,217 Janet Gordon of Auchinoun, m. 1493

18,432 Hugh Fraser, 1st Lord Lovat (1436-1501)
18,433 Margaret Lyon, m. c.1459

36,864 Thomas Fraser, 5th of Lovat (c.1417-1450)
36,865 Lady Janet Dunbar, m. 1433

73,728 Hugh Fraser, 4th of Lovat (1377-1440)
73,729 Janet Fenton of Beaufort, m. 1416

147,456 Alexander Fraser, 2nd Lovat, d. c.1416
147,457 Elizabeth Keith, m. c.1373

294,912 Hugh Fraser, 1st of Lovat, d. 1410
294,913 Isobel Wemyss of Wemyss

Charles Fraser, 4th Lord Fraser
(Cont'd.)

32 Andrew Fraser, 5th Muchalls, d. ante 1563
33 Margaret Irvine of Drum
48 Alexander Fraser, 4th Lord Lovat (1527-57)
49 Janet Campbell of Cawdor, m. c.1546
64 Andrew Fraser, 4th Muchalls, d.1549
65 Margaret Forbes
96 Hugh Fraser, 3rd Lord Lovat (c.1494-1544)
97 Janet Ross of Balnagowan, m. c.1526
128 Thomas Fraser, 3rd Muchalls, d. 1535
129 Miss Stewart
192 Thomas Fraser, 2nd Lord Lovat (1460-1524)
193 Janet Gordon of Auchindoun, m. 1493
256 Sir Andrew Fraser, 2nd Muchalls, d. 1505
257 Muriel Sutherland
384 Hugh Fraser, 1st Lord Lovat (1436-1501)
385 Margaret Lyon, m. c.1459
512 Thomas Fraser, 1st Muchalls, d. c.1475
513 Spouse of Thomas Fraser
768 Thomas Fraser, 5th Lovat (c.1417-1450)
769 Lady Janet Dunbar, m. 1433
1,024 Thomas Fraser of Cornton, d. c.1427
1,025 Spouse of Thomas Fraser
1,536 Hugh Fraser, 4th Lovat (1377-1440)
1,537 Janet Fenton of Beaufort, m. 1416
2,048 Thomas Fraser of Cornton, d. c.1392
2,049 Spouse of Thomas Fraser
3,072 Alexander Fraser, 2nd Lovat, d. c.1416
3,073 Elizabeth Keith, m. c.1373
4,096 ? Fraser of Cornton
4,097 Spouse of ? Fraser of Cornton
6,144 Hugh Fraser, 1st Lovat, d. 1410
6,145 Isobel Wemyss of Wemyss

Signatures of Lovat Frasers, Cadets

Simon Fraser, 6th Lord Lovat [1570-1633]
son of Hugh Fraser, 5th Lord Lovat
by wife Lady Elizabeth Stewart

Hugh Fraser, 7th Lord Lovat [1591-1645]
son of Simon Fraser, 6th Lord Lovat
by 1st wife Catherine Mackenzie of Kintail

Sir James Fraser of Brae [1612-1649]
Tutor of Lovat, son of Simon 6th Lord Lovat
by 2nd wife Jean Stewart

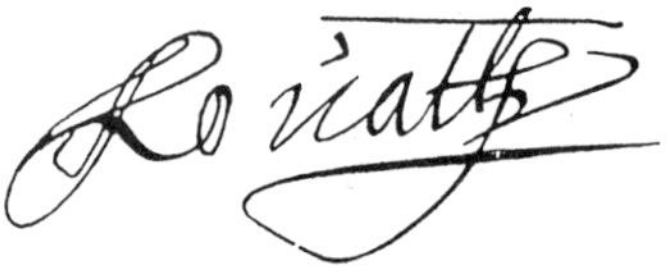

Hugh Fraser, 8th Lord Lovat [1642/3-1672]
only son of Hugh Fraser of Lovat
by wife Lady Ann Leslie of Leven

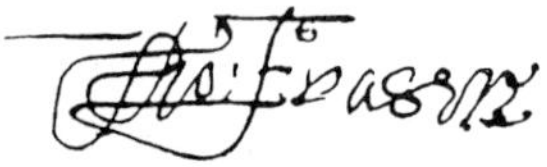

Thomas Fraser of Beaufort [1631-1699]
4th son of Hugh Fraser, 7th Lord Lovat
by wife Isobel Wemyss of Wemyss

Signatures: from The Old Lords of Lavat and Beaufort published in 1934, before the fire at Beaufort Castle. 15th Lord Lovat's signature from 1875 letter to the Hon. John Fraser

Mr James Fraser of Phopachy [1633/4-1705]
Minister, Kirkhill & Author of the *Wardlaw MS*
son of Wm Fraser, 2nd of Phopachy
by wife Alison Fraser of Tain

Maj James Fraser of CastleLeather [1670-1760]
Author of *Major Fraser's Manuscript*
son of Malcolm Fraser, 3rd of Culduthel
by 2nd wife Anna Baillie of Dunain

Simon Fraser, 11th Lord Lovat [1668-1747]
2nd son of Thomas Fraser of Beaufort
by wife Sybilla Macleod of Macleod

Simon Fraser, Master of Lovat [1726-1782]
eldest son of Simon Fraser, 11th Lord Lovat
by 1st wife Margaret Grant of Grant

Simon Fraser, 15th Lord Lovat [1818-1887]
son of Thomas Fraser, 14th Lord Lovat
by wife Charlotte Jerningham

[de Berry], grandson of Lieut. Malcolm Fraser [1733-1815] of Fraser's Highlanders, raised in 1757 by Col. Simon Fraser, who fought with Wolfe at Louisbourg & Quebec.

Tricentennial of Founding of Quebec - 1908
Standing: Col Turnbull, Msgr Mathieu, Lord Howick, Sir Robert Borden, Sir Wilfrid Laurier, Sir Charles Fitzpatrick, Lt-Gov Duncan Fraser, Msgr Laflamme, L.A. Taschereau. Sitting: Marquis de Lévis Mirepoix, Capt Arthur Murray, Comte Bernard de Montcalm, George Wolfe, Marquis de Lévis, Lord Lovat, Capt the Hon Dudley Carleton, Lord Bruce

Wedding *of*
Rosamund Broughton
and Lord Lovat

Beaufort Castle *high above the River Beauly.*
Built in the 1870s by the 15th Lord Lovat, the castle, with contents, was sold in 1995 to Mrs. Ann Gloag

Old 78th Fraser Highlanders

Inset: Colonel the Hon Simon Fraser, Master of Lovat. In 1757 he raised and commanded the 78th Highland Regiment of Foot [Fraser's Highlanders] who fought with Wolfe at Louisbourg and Quebec. Reconstituted for Expo 67 in Montreal, under the authority of Brigadier the Rt Hon Lord Lovat, 17th Lord Lovat and 24th Chief of Clan Fraser of Lovat, the Old 78th Fraser Highlanders Regiment was created as an historical re-enactment unit under the auspices of The Montreal Military & Maritime Museum [now known as The David M. Stewart Museum], with private funding. Garrisons and Outposts have since been formed across Canada and the United States.

Lord Lovat at home, writing his memoirs, in 1978

Lord Lovat, in his book *March Past*, recalled the bad fire in the east wing at Beaufort Castle before the Second World War, which destroyed the picture gallery, the ballroom, and the library, with all their treasures; also the billiard room, in which sporting trophies hung upon the walls.

Jack Fraser (later to serve in the Lovat Scouts), distinguished himself that night in the rescue operation, but not quite in the way that my mother expected. Scorning the family portraits by Allan Ramsay, Raeburn, and Sargent, all shriveling into flames, he dashed through the fire and smoke to the stuffed heads in the billiard room, further from the exit, seized a forty-eight-pound salmon (I think it stood next to my own sea trout), and returning through the blaze, triumphantly presented my mother with the hard-won prize.

Simon Fraser
University

Simon Fraser University Pipe Band

In 1965, Lord Lovat attended the official opening of Simon Fraser University in Vancouver, British Columbia, named after Simon Fraser the explorer. Lord Lovat allowed the University to use part of his personal coat of arms and adaptation of his motto 'je suis prest' as 'nous sommes prest'. The Simon Fraser University Pipe Band, who wear the Fraser tartan and Clan Fraser of Lovat badge, won the prestigious World Pipe Band Championship in Glasgow, Scotland in 1995 & 1996.

4

Clan Fraser

Two Chiefs

The Frasers of Philorth, Lords Saltoun, being the senior line, are Chiefs of the name of Fraser, although a Lowland family. Lord Lovat is chief of the very numerous Highland Clan Fraser of Lovat, based in Inverness-shire.

Many people are confused as to the relative positions of Lady Saltoun and Lord Lovat. It is not easy. Lady Saltoun is Chief of the name of Fraser, which is really just head of the family. That means that she is head of the senior line of Frasers extant in this country. People who are of Fraser blood are her kin. But Lord Lovat, who is descended from a younger brother of Sir Alexander Fraser, the Chamberlain, is Chief of Clan Fraser of Lovat, and many of the names associated with Clan Fraser, such as Sim and MacKimmie probably owe their allegiance in the first instance to him rather than to her, particularly if they are descended from *boll o' meal* Frasers, that is, people of other names who took the name of Fraser in return for land and food given to them by Lord Lovat. But then they or their descendants must, in many cases, have married people who were Frasers by blood. If they were living in Fraser country, they could not have helped doing so, in those days when people living 15 miles away were considered foreigners, and you did not marry into another clan unless it was improbable that there would ever be war between your clans.

So there is no way of being sure in a great many cases whether people are of the blood or not, but it is probable that many have a genuine Fraser descent, however, indirectly.

Many distinguished soldiers, sailors and airmen have been Frasers, and many settled in the United States of America and Canada after the war against the French in Quebec. Many others have emigrated to those countries and to Australia and New Zealand. There are Frasers in most countries in the world.

Arms and Mottoes

The Lady Saltoun, Chief of the name of Fraser

Reproduced with
the kind permission
of Debrett's Peerage Limited.

Arms:
Azure, three fraises or cinquefoils Argent

Crest:
Dexter, on a mount a flourish of strawberries leaved and fructed Proper

Motto:
Dexter, All my hope is in God

Supporters:
Two angels Proper with wings expanded and vested in long garments Or

Standard:
Azure, a St. Andrew's Cross Argent in the hoist and of the Livery Azure, upon which is depicted the Badge three times along with the Motto 'All my hope is in God' in letters Azure upon two transverse bands Argent

Pinsel:
Argent, on a Wreath of the Liveries the Crest as above, within a strap Azure, buckled and embellished Or inscribed in letters Argent 'All my hope is in God', all within a circlet Or fimbriated Gules and blazoned with the style 'Fraser, Lady Saltoun' in letters Azure, the circlet ensigned of a Lord of Parliament's coronet Proper, and in the fly a strawberry flower slipped and leaved Proper.

Badge:
A fraise Argent

These arms may only be used by Lady Saltoun

Lord Lovat, Chief of Clan Fraser of Lovat

I am ready.
JE
SUIS
PREST

Arms:
Quarterly, 1st & 4th, Azure, three fraises Argent (Fraser); 2nd & 3rd, Argent, three antique crowns Gules (Bisset)

Crest:
A buck's head erased Proper

Motto:
Je suis prest (I am ready)

Supporters:
Two bucks rampant Proper

These arms may only be used by Lord Lovat.

Reproduced with
the kind permission
of Debrett's Peerage Limited.

Crest Badges

The Court of the Lord Lyon states that the popular name *Clan Crest* is a misnomer, as there is no such thing as a *Clan Crest.* The Crest is the exclusive **personal** property of the Clan Chief, and it is fully protected to him/her by the law in Scotland.

Badges which may be used by Clansmen

ALL·MY·HOPE·IS·IN·GOD

Fraser

JE·SUIS·PREST

Fraser of Lovat

The definition of *Clansmen* [or *Clanswomen*] covers the Chief's relatives, including his/her own immediate family, and ALL members of the extended family called the *Clan*, whether bearing the Clan surname or that of one of its Septs; *in sum*, all those who profess allegiance to that Chief and wish to demonstrate their association with the Clan.

It is correct for these to wear their Chief's Crest encircled with a STRAP AND BUCKLE bearing their Chief's Motto or Slogan. The strap and buckle is the sign of the clansman, and he demonstrates his membership of his Chief's Clan by wearing his Chief's Crest within it. Although the Crest Badge is purchased by and is therefore owned by the clansman, the heraldic Crest and Motto on it belong to the Chief and NOT to the clansman. They are the Chief's exclusive heraldic property, which the clansman is only thus permitted to wear.

Flags

At Highland Games in Canada, the United States, Australia or elsewhere, where other Clans are present, it is proper to display flags which show the Clan Fraser *Clansmen's* Crest Badge, comprising the Chief's Crest within a strap and buckle inscribed with the Motto or Slogan, although the name of the Clan should *not* be added, as Clansmen should know their own Crest Badge. The flag may be either a *Banner* [flown from a vertical pole attached to one side of it] or a *Gonfanon* [suspended from a horizontal cross bar along its top edge]. The authority for its display at any time and place resides in the Chief alone. However, it is *not* correct to use the *Banner* or *Gonfanon* in the presence of the Chief, only when the Chief is not present. The standard may only be used by the Chief, and the same applies to any flag bearing the PLAIN ARMS.

Who is a Member of Clan Fraser?

The families listed below are either of Fraser descent or are descended from dependents of the Frasers. Fraser and Frizzell are thought to be variants of the same name by most sources and there is evidence of this in old charters. Incidentally, the spelling of names and, in fact, of all words was a very haphazard affair in times gone by (and often still is) and different spellings of Fraser, Frizzell, MacKimmie and Simon should merely be regarded as different ways of indicating on paper the same name, or the same sound.

Simon is the preferred name for the Chief of Clan Fraser of Lovat, certainly in modern times, but is very common in most branches of the family at all times throughout history.

So, illegitimate children of Lovat Chiefs, or indeed of any Fraser, whose name was Simon, would be quite likely to be given Simon, MacSimon, Sim or Simpson or one of their variants as a surname. But then one has to remember that the Christian name *Simon* was not exclusive to the Fraser family! A certain amount would depend on what part of the country the family came from, that is to say that a MacSimon from the area round Beauly in Inverness-shire would be much more likely to descend from a Fraser of Lovat than one from some other part of the country.

All in all, it is impossible to be precise as to who is or is not of Fraser descent, for, apart from anything else, too many records have been lost. But if someone writes to Lady Saltoun or Lord Lovat and greets them as the head of his family, they don't say *Produce your pedigree and prove it.* They say *welcome, kinsman*, whether his name be Fraser or Tweedie or any of the others on that list, which does not include *all* known spellings of those names!

List of Fraser Sept Names

In addition to Fraser, many other surnames are associated with our clan, known as *Septs*. A surname can be associated with more than one clan, depending upon the area in which they lived. Some of these names, and variations in spelling thereof, are included as follows:

Bissett Brewster Cowie Frizell Frew

Macgruer Mackim Mackimmie Macsimon Mactavish

Oliver Sim Simon Simpson Sims Syme Twaddle Tweedie

Tartans

There is a hunting Fraser which has a brown ground, and is usually worn during the day, and dress Fraser which has a red ground, and is for evening wear. Hunting Fraser may be worn in the evening for informal occasions, but it is unusual to wear dress Fraser during the day. There are various versions of these, but rarer versions are not commonly obtainable, so no-one need worry unduly when buying tartan.

Tartan Tidbits *[extracted from Highland Dress for Women below]*

Like the cut and origins of the kilt, the design and provenance of the patterns known as tartan are highly contentious. [*Collin's Encyclopaedia of Scotland*, 1994, edited by John Keay & Julia Keay]

Colonel Archibald Campbell Fraser [1736-1815], who succeeded his half-brother General Simon Fraser [1726-1782] in the Lovat estates, on his first appearance in the House of Commons in 1782, played an important role in supporting the motion by the Marquis of Graham [later Duke of Montrose] for the Repeal of the *Unclothing Act* and legalising the use of the Highland dress.

Although they cannot agree on the origins, most scholars and historians credit the influential novelist and poet Sir Walter Scott [1771-1832] with romanticizing the history of tartans. Scott, along with General Stewart of Garth, masterminded the state visit of George IV, who became the first reigning monarch to visit Scotland since the time of Charles II. King George IV appeared in kilt and plaid for the royal visit in 1822, for which William Wilson & Sons of Bannockburn manufactured about 150 tartans.

Enter two brothers, John Sobieski Stolberg Stuart [c.1795-1872] and Charles Edward Stuart [c.1799-1880], who arrived in Scotland, claiming to be grandsons and heirs of Prince Charles Edward [1720-1788]. Thomas Fraser, 10th of Strichen [1802-1875] who had in 1837 been created Baron Lovat in the Peerage of the United Kingdom [and in 1857 became 14th Lord Lovat] listened sympathetically to their claims and indulged their pretension.

In 1838 he built a house for the brothers on the 60 acre island of Eilean Aigas in the middle of the Beauly river, where they learned Gaelic and produced several collections of verse. In 1842 the Sobieski Stuart brothers published their *ancient* work on clan tartans *Vestiarium Scoticum*, which formed the basis for the development of modern tartan. Although now regarded more for its inventiveness than authenticity, it nevertheless was received with enthusiasm by the public and the manufacturers who were quite willing to satisfy the increasing demand for tartans and to support the argument that they need not be restricted to a particular clan.

The trend started by George IV was continued by Queen Victoria and her husband Prince Albert who, during a holiday at Balmoral in 1852, purchased an Aberdeenshire estate, commissioned a new castle to be built on the site and designed a tartan to be the exclusive property of the Royal Family.

Several books on Scottish Tartans have proclaimed that *Tartan is too attractive to be confined to Scotland*, and the rest of the world agrees. Today there are in excess of 2,000 registered tartans, according to the *Scottish Tartans Authority*.

Highland Dress for Men *[by W. Neil Fraser]*

Wearing the Kilt - Correctly

Having worn the Kilt since the age of 7, and at least weekly from the age of 12 to 20 as a Drummer in the Seaforth Highlanders of Canada Cadet Corp in British Columbia, I learned to feel very comfortable in the traditional dress of Highland Scots. In recent years, I have worn the Kilt frequently at many Scottish events in Ontario. With the fall social season in full swing, and *Fraser Week at Castle Fraser* approaching, it occurred to me that I should share some of my experience with fellow CFSNA members, who may be donning the Kilt for the first time, and are unsure of how to wear things correctly. The Kilt we wear today is a modern adaptation of the ancient Highland version. The *fealeadh beg* (anglicized to philibeg, or little kilt) is the tailored style which covers only from the waist to the knee. The philibeg also solves the problem of having to pleat it every morning, as the pleats are permanently stitched in place and pressed.

Having endured the wrath of the odd Sergeant Major as a recruit in the Seaforths about how not to wear my Kilt, I had to learn the rules rather quickly. The hem should be just at the break of the kneecap and, if the Kilt is properly tailored for you, it should be symmetrical front and back (not drooping at the rear).

The best test for length is to kneel on the floor, and the hem should just touch the floor. Most Kilts have three belts, one on the left which fits through a slot, and two on the right to keep the apron tight. It should go without saying, that the pleats are at the back, but I have seen photos of some very prominent people wearing the Kilt backwards (supposedly, to keep the pleats neater).

The Correct Tartan

Most men who plan to wear the Kilt only invest in one. I say *invest*, because a good quality kilt is quite expensive, and quality is far more important than quantity. Frasers have a variety of Tartans to choose from, in many variations of shade and colour. Probably the wisest choice for a first Kilt is a Red Fraser, but you can select one of the colour variations which try to emulate the older faded red look if you want to be different. The general rule is that Red Fraser Tartan is only worn in the evening, usually with formal wear. For day wear, Hunting Fraser (with a brown ground) is really the correct Tartan, if you get carried away and buy two Kilts. My preference is Ancient Hunting Fraser, which has a light brown ground with bright green and blue squares. Since most of us wear the Kilt mainly for evening events, you won't be censured for wearing Red Fraser in the daytime, as long as it is worn properly!

From the Bottom

Now that you have a Kilt, you will need some basic accoutrements to wear with it. Let's start with kilt hose (long stockings). With formal dress, matching Tartan Hose are appropriate, but they are very expensive. Most men prefer to wear white wool hose (really an off-white) for evening wear, with fold-down tops and elastic garter flashes, either in matching Tartan or plain red. Shoes can be the traditional Ghillie Brogues, with open lacing area and long tasseled laces wrapped around the ankle and lower calf, tied slightly off to the side just below the calf. For evening wear, I prefer patent leather formal shoes with a square Silver buckle. To complete the ensemble, most wear a *Sgian Dubh* (Anglicized as Skean Dhu) or small sheathed black knife, often crested with a Cairngorm stone, tucked into the side at the top of the right stocking.

The Middle

The sporran is an essential part of Highland garb, which has few pockets, to carry your wallet, money, etc. Sporrans come in an endless variety, but fall into two basic categories, dress for evening wear and less fancy leather for day wear. Dress sporrans usually have some sort of fur (Sealskin is common) with matching tassels, crested with a Silver hasp. The purse is usually at the back of the sporran with a fastener to open and close it. Cost can vary from a few hundred dollars (white metal) to a few thousand (Sterling Silver). The best way to tell it is Silver, is that it tarnishes and has to be polished regularly, so save your money.

Many men also wear a wide black leather belt with large silver buckle, but it is more common to wear a belt with a day jacket than with a formal evening jacket. Belt buckles come in a wide variety of plain, clan crested and various Celtic designs, and vary in cost. Silver is very expensive, and needs polishing.

Above the Kilt - Evening Wear

For formal evening wear (the most common reason to own all this expensive stuff), most men prefer a Black Prince Charlie Formal Jacket with matching vest. Both jacket and vest have diamond shaped buttons, usually in white metal, but Silver plated on better quality jackets. Also common is the doublet style jacket, similar to those worn by pipe bands, (without all the gold or silver braid). Most prefer to wear a formal dress shirt and black bow tie, but the more flamboyant may want to wear the Jabot style shirt with lace front and cuffs (just keep the cuffs out of the soup). If you really want to stand out, you can opt for a velvet jacket in dark green or blue with the lace front and cuffs (skip the powdered wig).

Once you get the hang of it, you will have more fun than the *Penguin Patrol,* so common at black tie events, and leave no doubt of your Scottish ancestry and heritage.

Less common today, but making a comeback, is the Tartan Shoulder Plaid. I prefer the half plaid, pinned at the shoulder with a plaid brooch (usually Silver with a large Cairngorm or other semi-precious stone) draping at the back to the bottom of the Kilt, and just short of the waist at the front. The full plaid, like those worn by pipers, is too hot for most indoor venues, as it is wrapped diagonally from shoulder to waist, front and back, pinned at the shoulder and falls almost to the floor at the back.

Above the Kilt - Day Wear

A day jacket is more of a personal choice, much as one would choose a sports jacket or less formal business suit. A popular choice for Frasers is a tweed in either Lovat Green or Lovat Blue, but Harris, Houndstooth or Herringbone Tweeds are also available. Day jackets are usually called Argyle Jackets, and resemble what we call a sports jacket, but shorter, and the front is rounded to show the sporran. The shoulders often have twisted cord epaulets.

Matching or contrasting vests may also be worn in cooler weather. Buttons are usually made of horn, with three buttons on the face of the sleeve and pocket flaps, and on the shoulder epaulets. Shirts can be as varied as you choose, but button-down coloured or checked shirts are common. Many men wear Tartan ties, but it is more correct to wear a plain Green or Blue woolen tie, or a Regimental or Club tie, with a day jacket.

Headgear

Skip the headgear with formal evening wear. Not only is wearing a hat indoors frowned upon, a hat is a damn nuisance if you have to tuck it into your Kilt or under your shoulder epaulet all evening. For day wear, the two main choices are a Glengarry (wedge cap), usually black with either a diced or plain band, or a Balmoral (round flat Tam-O-Shanter), available in a variety of colours; black, pale green, pale blue or tan, with either diced or plain headband. It is common to leave the black ribbon tails on a Glengarry, but most prefer a Balmoral with just a small bow at the back of the headband, rather than the trailing ribbons. It is common to wear a Belted Clan Crest Badge on either headgear, pinned onto the black cockade (pleated ribbon) at the left front side. Frasers have both the Saltoun Crest Badge (Fraser) or Lovat Crest Badge (Fraser of Lovat) to choose from.

Skip the feathers, which mean something in Highland Custom, and *should never be worn* unless you are entitled to do so. Any book on Scottish Heraldry and Highland Tradition will explain the hierarchy. Scots take such customs *very seriously*, and we don't want you to get tossed into the Castle Fraser dungeon!

Arming Yourself

Once you feel comfortable wearing traditional Highland dress, you may want to experiment with some variations on the basic accoutrements. Some opt for the next level of decorative Highland weapon, *The Dirk*. The dirk was a second line of defense, after the sword. There are many beautifully crafted and decorated dirks available, but most are very expensive. The dirk is worn on the belt at the right side of the Kilt. The dirk was a combination weapon/mess kit for the Highland warriors.

Wearing a Basket Hilt Sword is not only awkward to manage in tight quarters, but the chances of being challenged to a duel are getting less common. If you enjoy Highland weaponry, the Royal Canadian Military Institute [my club in Toronto] has enough swords to satisfy anyone's curiosity, but leave your ancestor's favourite weapons at home in the display case.

A little practice in sitting is in order, lest you reveal more than you intend. Try backing into the chair while keeping the pleats of your Kilt even, and press the apron and sporran down between the knees before sitting. With a little practice, you will get the hang of it, so to speak.

Highland Underwear

Very difficult to describe - due to scarcity of evidence.

Highland Dress for Women *[by Marie Fraser]*

Unlike my husband, my exposure to Scots and Highland dress came rather late in life. So, I was a bit surprised when Neil decided that I should prepare a companion piece to his leaflet on *The Rules for Wearing the Kilt.* The subject is a minefield for us lassies [wives, mothers, girlfriends], especially if you try to follow the many conflicting guidelines in various published articles and illustrated brochures on Highland ladies wear and accessories. Many of these have been devised by men who are, after all, trying to make an honest living from the mystique and overwhelming success of recent Hollywood movies like *Rob Roy*, *Braveheart*, *The Bruce* and *Loch Ness.*

Ladies, if you want to maintain a happy and harmonious relationship with your loved ones:
(a) don't refer to your kilt skirt as a kilt [only men wear kilts], and
(b) don't try to outshine your partner.

Lady Saltoun's comments on Highland dress for women are very much appreciated:

(1) "Women should not wear kilts! They should wear skirts, the design of which may follow the current fashion." Skirts can be -
   (a) designed rather like a kilt,
   (b) straight,
   (c) with knife pleats all round,
   (d) with box pleats or inverted pleats, or
   (e) circular, cut on the cross.

   Women can also wear tartan trousers or tartan shorts in summer, preferably in silk!

(2) "For formal day wear a jacket of plain cloth in one of the colours in the tartan looks nice, with a matching or toning blouse or sweater. No sporrans, please - just a normal handbag, and simple shoes and stockings in the fashion of the day. Hats, if at all, should be simple and chosen to suit the wearer." [So, if you fell for the fancy sporran slung over the model's shoulders in the Highland ladies wear catalogue, remember that the shopkeeper can always claim he thought you were buying it for your favourite man.]

(3) "All the mystique about how sashes should be worn is a lot of hooey! I have generally worn mine over my left shoulder, crossing on the shoulder with the ends hanging down, and fastened with a brooch. If you are left-handed, you may find it more convenient to wear it over the right shoulder."

> "Both the late Lady Erroll and I used sometimes to wear ours round our waists, and so did my daughters, although not to dance in the set reels at the Caledonian Ball in London, or for a very formal occasion." [The late Countess of Erroll (1926-78) was Lord High Constable of Scotland.]

"If you like to have a tartan evening dress or skirt, why not? One thing I would say: if you are going to wear a sash, *please* choose a *plain* dress, not patterned in any way, and in either black, white, cream or yellow, or one of the colours in the tartan. For example, dark green looks very well with dress Fraser, or dark blue." [Red, unless it is an exact match, should be avoided, and anyway you risk being labeled *The Scarlet Woman*.]

The Price of Highland Dress

It can cost £1,000 or more to outfit your man for evening wear, and slightly less for day wear. So, you have considerable leeway in choosing what to wear with that tartan sash, to accompany your male Highland peacock!

Dress Kilt	£ 300
Evening Jacket	250
Dress Shirt	30
Bow Tie	7
Dress Shoes	100
Stockings & Flashes	95
Dress Sporran	160 +
Skean Dhu	45 +
Kilt Pin	21 +

Music

Several songs, ballads and musical scores have been associated with the Fraser name over the years. Alexander MacDonald wrote *An Elegy on Lord Lovat* after the execution in London in 1747 of the 11th Lord Lovat [a Whig in 1715 and a Jacobite in 1745], who had been condemned and sentenced by his peers after impeachment by the House of Commons. For the first annual gathering of the Clan Fraser in Canada in 1894, Georgina Fraser Newhall wrote *Fraser's Drinking Song*, with music by J. Lewis Browne. In addition to *Lady Saltoun's Reel* and *Lord Saltoun's Reel*, there is *Lord Lovat's Lament* [as a march], and more recently, *The Gathering of Clan Fraser*, composed by Pipe Major Chris Stevens for the inaugural meeting of the Clan Fraser Society of New Zealand in 1993.

Tracing Your Ancestors

This is a very time consuming business if you are going to do it yourself, but very rewarding. Many helpful books have been published on the subject. If you cannot do it yourself, you can employ a professional researcher to do it for you. But you do have to be able to provide your researcher with a certain amount of basic information, otherwise he/she will not be able to help you, and you will be wasting your money. For an idea of what sort of information you need, Base 7 of *Scottish Roots*, by Alwn James, is helpful.

There are quite a number of organisations offering to do ancestral research at a price. Some are far from reputable, and have been known to tell people a load of rubbish and charged the earth for it.

The growth of interest in genealogy and *roots* has produced a rash of cowboys in this field, in business for what they can get out of it, and none too particular about the accuracy of the information they pretend they have discovered.

A list of independent research agents located in Scotland and the United Kingdom can be obtained through the various Clan Fraser societies in Australia, New Zealand, Canada, the U.S.A. or Scotland and the United Kingdom.

The Early Frasers

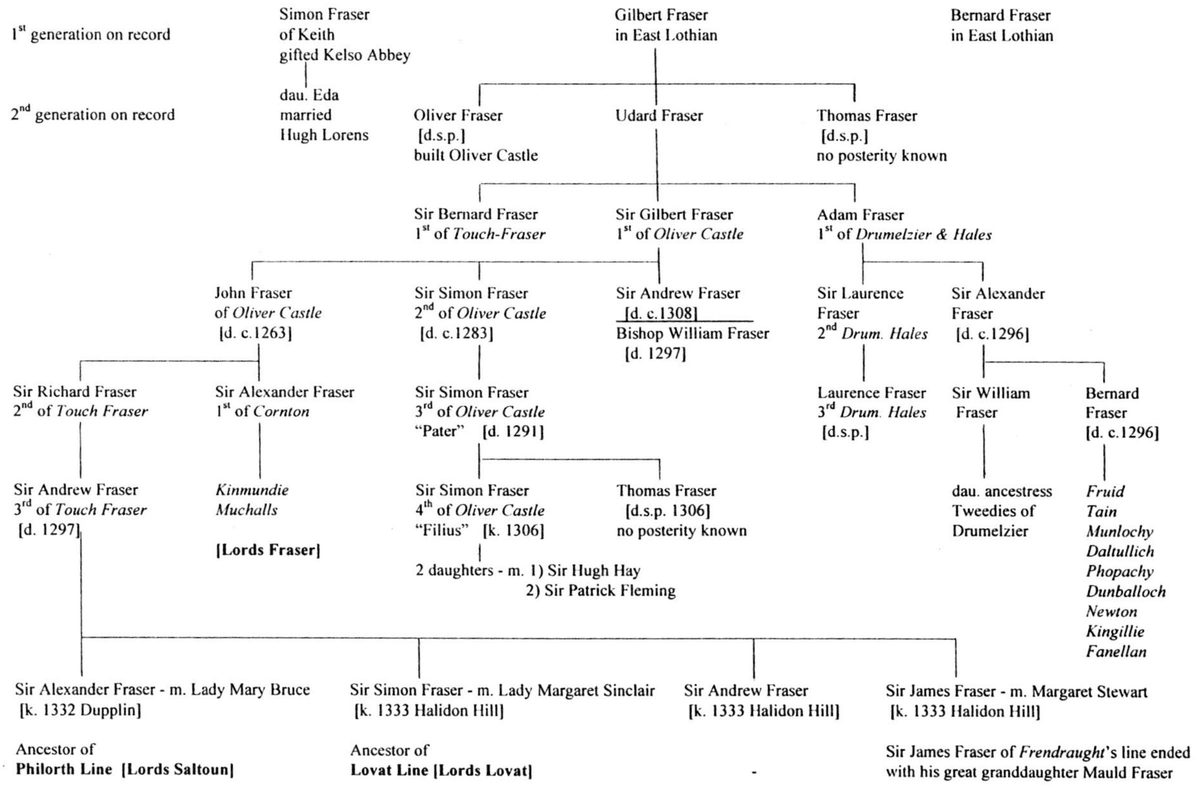
1st generation on record
2nd generation on record
Simon Fraser
of Keith
gifted Kelso Abbey
dau. Eda
married
Hugh Lorens
Gilbert Fraser
in East Lothian
Bernard Fraser
in East Lothian
Oliver Fraser
[d.s.p.]
built Oliver Castle
Udard Fraser
Thomas Fraser
[d.s.p.]
no posterity known
Sir Bernard Fraser
1st of Touch-Fraser
Sir Gilbert Fraser
1st of Oliver Castle
Adam Fraser
1st of Drumelzier & Hales
John Fraser
of Oliver Castle
[d. c.1263]
Sir Simon Fraser
2nd of Oliver Castle
[d. c.1283]
Sir Andrew Fraser
[d. c.1308]
Bishop William Fraser
[d. 1297]
Sir Laurence
Fraser
2nd Drum. Hales
Sir Alexander
Fraser
[d. c.1296]
Sir Richard Fraser
2nd of Touch Fraser
Sir Alexander Fraser
1st of Cornton
Sir Simon Fraser
3rd of Oliver Castle
"Pater" [d. 1291]
Laurence Fraser
3rd Drum. Hales
[d.s.p.]
Sir William
Fraser
Bernard
Fraser
[d. c.1296]
Sir Andrew Fraser
3rd of Touch Fraser
[d. 1297]
Kinmundie
Muchalls
[Lords Fraser]
Sir Simon Fraser
4th of Oliver Castle
"Filius" [k. 1306]
Thomas Fraser
[d.s.p. 1306]
no posterity known
dau. ancestress
Tweedies of
Drumelzier
Fruid
Tain
Munlochy
Daltullich
Phopachy
Dunballoch
Newton
Kingillie
Fanellan
2 daughters - m. 1) Sir Hugh Hay
2) Sir Patrick Fleming
Sir Alexander Fraser - m. Lady Mary Bruce
[k. 1332 Dupplin]
Sir Simon Fraser - m. Lady Margaret Sinclair
[k. 1333 Halidon Hill]
Sir Andrew Fraser
[k. 1333 Halidon Hill]
Sir James Fraser - m. Margaret Stewart
[k. 1333 Halidon Hill]
Ancestor of
Philorth Line [Lords Saltoun]
Ancestor of
Lovat Line [Lords Lovat]
-
Sir James Fraser of Frendraught's line ended
with his great granddaughter Mauld Fraser

The Frasers of Philorth - Lords Saltoun

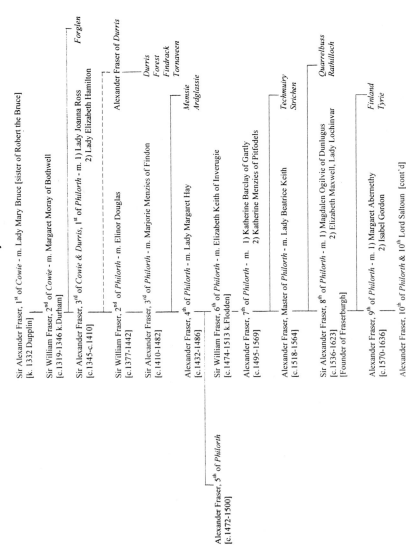

Sir Alexander Fraser, 1st of *Cowie* - m. Lady Mary Bruce [sister of Robert the Bruce]
[k. 1332 Dupplin]

Sir William Fraser, 2nd of *Cowie* - m. Margaret Moray of Bothwell
[c.1319-1346 k.Durham]

Sir Alexander Fraser, 3rd of *Cowie & Durris*, 1st of *Philorth* - m. 1) Lady Joanna Ross
2) Lady Elizabeth Hamilton
[c.1345-c.1410]
— *Forglen*
— Alexander Fraser of *Durris*: *Durris*, *Forest*, *Findrack*, *Tornaveen*

Sir William Fraser, 2nd of *Philorth* - m. Elinor Douglas
[c.1377-1442]

Sir Alexander Fraser, 3rd of *Philorth* - m. Marjorie Menzies of Findon
[c.1410-1482]
— *Memsie*, *Ardglassie*

Alexander Fraser, 4th of *Philorth* - m. Lady Margaret Hay
[c.1432-1486]
— Alexander Fraser, 5th of *Philorth* [c.1472-1500]

Sir William Fraser, 6th of *Philorth* - m. Elizabeth Keith of Inverugie
[c.1474-1513 k.Flodden]

Alexander Fraser, 7th of *Philorth* - m. 1) Katherine Barclay of Gartly
2) Katherine Menzies of Pitfodels
[c.1495-1569]
— *Techmuiry*, *Strichen*

Alexander Fraser, Master of *Philorth* - m. Lady Beatrice Keith
[c.1518-1564]
— *Quarrelbuss*, *Rathilloch*

Sir Alexander Fraser, 8th of *Philorth* - m. 1) Magdalen Ogilvie of Dunlugus
2) Elizabeth Maxwell, Lady Lochinvar
[c.1536-1623]
[Founder of Fraserburgh]
— *Finland*, *Tyrie*

Alexander Fraser, 9th of *Philorth* - m. 1) Margaret Abernethy
2) Isabel Gordon
[c.1570-1636]

Alexander Fraser, 10th of *Philorth* & 10th Lord Saltoun [cont'd]

The Frasers of Philorth - Lords Saltoun

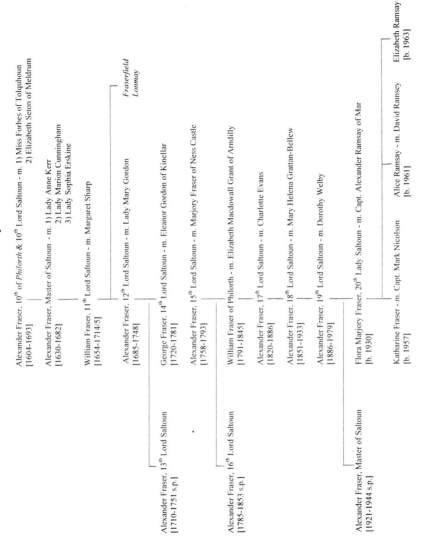

Alexander Fraser, 10th of *Philorth* & 10th Lord Saltoun - m. 1) Miss Forbes of Tolquhoun
[1604-1693] 2) Elizabeth Seton of Meldrum

Alexander Fraser, Master of Saltoun - m. 1) Lady Anne Kerr
[1630-1682] 2) Lady Marion Cunningham
3) Lady Sophia Erskine

William Fraser, 11th Lord Saltoun - m. Margaret Sharp
[1654-1714/5]

Alexander Fraser, 12th Lord Saltoun - m. Lady Mary Gordon
[1685-1748]

Fraserfield
Lonmay

Alexander Fraser, 13th Lord Saltoun
[1710-1751 s.p.]

George Fraser, 14th Lord Saltoun - m. Eleanor Gordon of Kinellar
[1720-1781]

Alexander Fraser, 15th Lord Saltoun - m. Marjory Fraser of Ness Castle
[1758-1793]

Alexander Fraser, 16th Lord Saltoun
[1785-1853 s.p.]

William Fraser of Philorth - m. Elizabeth Macdowall Grant of Arndilly
[1791-1845]

Alexander Fraser, 17th Lord Saltoun - m. Charlotte Evans
[1820-1886]

Alexander Fraser, 18th Lord Saltoun - m. Mary Helena Grattan-Bellew
[1851-1933]

Alexander Fraser, 19th Lord Saltoun - m. Dorothy Welby
[1886-1979]

Alexander Fraser, Master of Saltoun
[1921-1944 s.p.]

Flora Marjory Fraser, 20th Lady Saltoun - m. Capt. Alexander Ramsay of Mar
[b. 1930]

Katharine Fraser - m. Capt. Mark Nicolson
[b. 1957]

Alice Ramsay - m. David Ramsey
[b. 1961]

Elizabeth Ramsay
[b. 1963]

The Frasers of Lovat - Lords Lovat

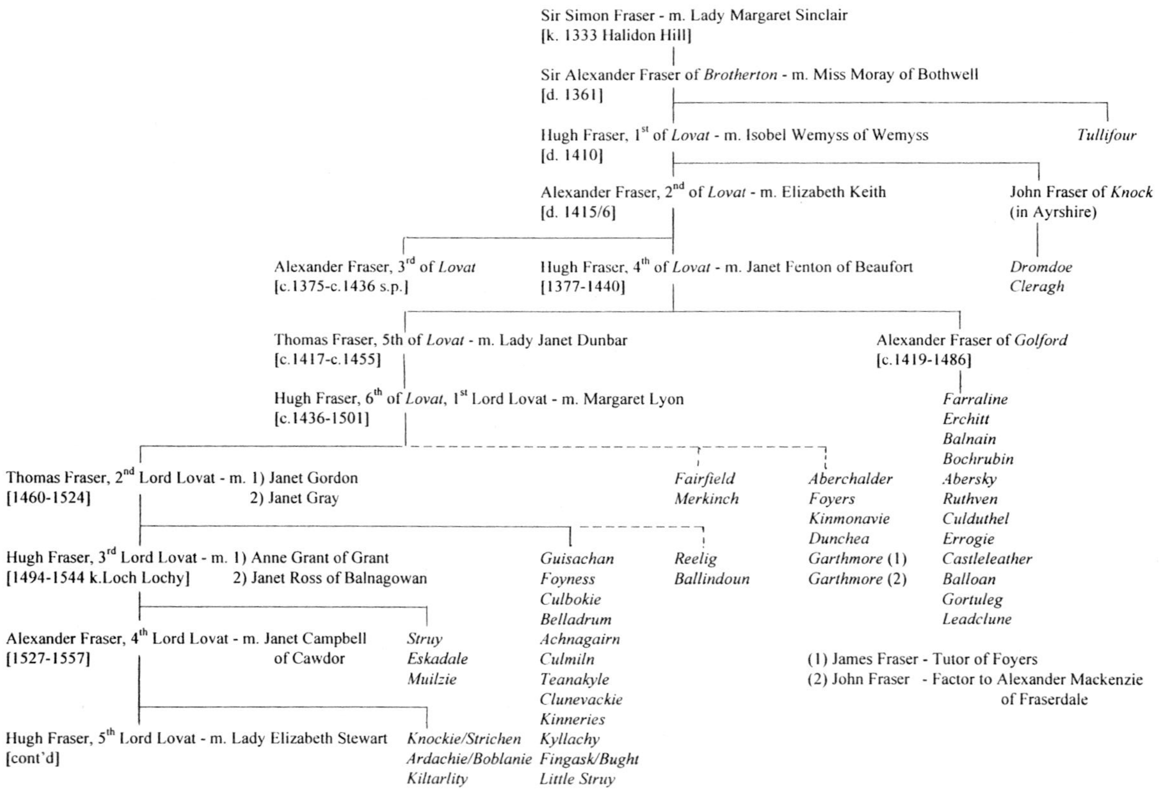
Sir Simon Fraser - m. Lady Margaret Sinclair
[k. 1333 Halidon Hill]
Sir Alexander Fraser of *Brotherton* - m. Miss Moray of Bothwell
[d. 1361]
Tullifour
Hugh Fraser, 1st of *Lovat* - m. Isobel Wemyss of Wemyss
[d. 1410]
John Fraser of *Knock*
(in Ayrshire)
Dromdoe
Cleragh
Alexander Fraser, 2nd of *Lovat* - m. Elizabeth Keith
[d. 1415/6]
Alexander Fraser, 3rd of *Lovat*
[c.1375-c.1436 s.p.]
Hugh Fraser, 4th of *Lovat* - m. Janet Fenton of Beaufort
[1377-1440]
Thomas Fraser, 5th of *Lovat* - m. Lady Janet Dunbar
[c.1417-c.1455]
Alexander Fraser of *Golford*
[c.1419-1486]
Farraline
Erchitt
Balnain
Bochrubin
Abersky
Ruthven
Culduthel
Errogie
Castleleather
Balloan
Gortuleg
Leadclune
Hugh Fraser, 6th of *Lovat*, 1st Lord Lovat - m. Margaret Lyon
[c.1436-1501]
Fairfield
Merkinch
Aberchalder
Foyers
Kinmonavie
Dunchea
Garthmore (1)
Garthmore (2)
Thomas Fraser, 2nd Lord Lovat - m. 1) Janet Gordon
2) Janet Gray
[1460-1524]
Reelig
Ballindoun
Hugh Fraser, 3rd Lord Lovat - m. 1) Anne Grant of Grant
2) Janet Ross of Balnagowan
[1494-1544 k.Loch Lochy]
Guisachan
Foyness
Culbokie
Belladrum
Achnagairn
Culmiln
Teanakyle
Clunevackie
Kinneries
Kyllachy
Fingask/Bught
Little Struy
Alexander Fraser, 4th Lord Lovat - m. Janet Campbell of Cawdor
[1527-1557]
Struy
Eskadale
Muilzie
Hugh Fraser, 5th Lord Lovat - m. Lady Elizabeth Stewart
[cont'd]
Knockie/Strichen
Ardachie/Boblanie
Kiltarlity
(1) James Fraser - Tutor of Foyers
(2) John Fraser - Factor to Alexander Mackenzie of Fraserdale

The Frasers of Lovat - Lords Lovat

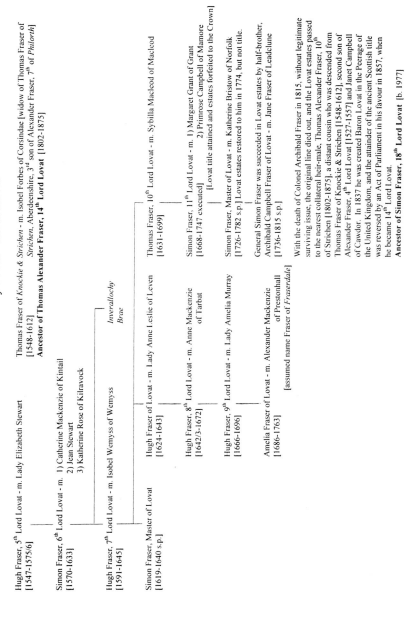

Hugh Fraser, 5th Lord Lovat - m. Lady Elizabeth Stewart
[1547-1575/6]

Thomas Fraser of *Knockie & Strichen* - m. Isobel Forbes of Corsindae [widow of Thomas Fraser of
[1548-1612] *Strichen*, Aberdeenshire, 3rd son of Alexander Fraser, 7th of *Philorth*]
Ancestor of Thomas Alexander Fraser, 14th Lord Lovat [1802-1875]

Simon Fraser, 6th Lord Lovat - m. 1) Catherine Mackenzie of Kintail
[1570-1633]
2) Jean Stewart
3) Katherine Rose of Kilravock

Hugh Fraser, 7th Lord Lovat - m. Isobel Wemyss of Wemyss
[1591-1645]

Inverallochy
Brae

Simon Fraser, Master of Lovat
[1619-1640 s.p.]

Hugh Fraser of Lovat - m. Lady Anne Leslie of Leven
[1624-1643]

Hugh Fraser, 8th Lord Lovat - m. Anne Mackenzie of Tarbat
[1642/3-1672]

Hugh Fraser, 9th Lord Lovat - m. Lady Amelia Murray
[1666-1696]

Amelia Fraser of Lovat - m. Alexander Mackenzie of Prestonhall
[1686-1763]
[assumed name Fraser of *Fraserdale*]

Thomas Fraser, 10th Lord Lovat - m. Sybilla Macleod of Macleod
[1631-1699]

Simon Fraser, 11th Lord Lovat - m. 1) Margaret Grant of Grant
[1668-1747 executed]
2) Primrose Campbell of Mamore
[Lovat title attained and estates forfeited to the Crown]

Simon Fraser, Master of Lovat - m. Katherine Bristow of Norfolk
[1726-1782 s.p.] Lovat estates restored to him in 1774, but not title.

General Simon Fraser was succeeded in Lovat estates by half-brother,
Archibald Campbell Fraser of Lovat - m. Jane Fraser of Leadclune
[1736-1815 s.p.]

With the death of Colonel Archibald Fraser in 1815, without legitimate surviving issue, the original line died out, and the Lovat estates passed to the nearest collateral heir-male, Thomas Alexander Fraser, 10th of Strichen [1802-1875], a distant cousin who was descended from Thomas Fraser of Knockie & Strichen [1548-1612], second son of Alexander Fraser, 4th Lord Lovat [1527-1557] and Janet Campbell of Cawdor. In 1837 he was created Baron Lovat in the Peerage of the United Kingdom, and the attainder of the ancient Scottish title was reversed by an Act of Parliament in his favour in 1857, when he became 14th Lord Lovat.
Ancestor of Simon Fraser, 18th Lord Lovat [b. 1977]

The Frasers of Lovat - Lords Lovat

Thomas Fraser of *Knockie & Strichen* - m. Isobel Forbest of Corsindae

Thomas Fraser, 2nd of *Strichen* - m. 1) Christian Forbes of Tolquhoun
[c.1582-1644/5] 2) Margaret Macleod

Thomas Fraser, 3rd of *Strichen* - m. Christian Forbes of Pitsligo
[1612-1656]

Thomas Fraser, 4th of *Strichen* - m. Marion Irvine of Fedderat
[c.1630-1685]

Alexander Fraser, 5th of *Strichen* - m. 1) Elizabeth Cockburn of Ormiston
[c.1659-1699] 2) Amelia Stewart

James Fraser, 6th of *Strichen*
[c.1698-1723 s.p.]

Alexander Fraser, 7th of *Strichen* - m. Lady Ann Campbell, Countess of Bute
[c.1699-1775]

Alexander Fraser, 8th of *Strichen* - m. Jean Menzies
[c.1733-1794]

Alexander Fraser, 9th of *Strichen* - m. Amelia Leslie of Balquhain
[1765-1803]

Thomas Alexander Fraser, 10th of *Strichen*, 14th Lord Lovat - m. Charlotte Jerningham
[1802-1875]

Simon Fraser, 15th Lord Lovat - m. Alice Mary Weld Blundell
[1828-1887]

Simon Fraser, Master of Lovat
[1867-1868]

Simon Fraser, 16th Lord Lovat - m. Laura Lister
[1871-1933]

Moniack

Simon Fraser, 17th Lord Lovat - m. Rosamund Broughton
[1911-1995]

Simon Fraser, Master of Lovat
[1939-1994] - m. Virginia Grose

Fiona Fraser [b.1941]
m. Richard Allen

Tessa Fraser [b.1942]
m. 1) Hugh Mackay, Lord Reay
2) Henry Keswick

Kim Fraser [b.1946]
m. Joanna North

Hugh Fraser [b.1947]
m. Druscilla Montgomerie

Andrew Fraser [1952-1994]
m. Lady Charlotte Greville

Simon Fraser, 18th Lord Lovat [b. 1977] Violet Fraser [b.1972] Honor Fraser [b.1973] Jack Fraser [b.1984]

Bibliography

Anderson, John, *Historical Account of the Family of Frisel or Fraser*, Edinburgh: W. Blackwood, 1825.

Fairrie, Angus, *The Northern Meeting 1788-1988*, Edinburgh: The Pentland Press, 1988.

Fergusson, Alexander, *Major Fraser's Manuscript*, 2 Volumes, Edinburgh: David Douglas, 1889.

Fraser, Alexander, 17th Lord Saltoun, *The Frasers of Philorth; Lords Saltoun*, 3 Volumes, Edinburgh: Privately printed, 1879.

Fraser, Alexander, *The Clan Fraser in Canada; A Souvenir of the First Annual Gathering, Toronto, May 5, 1894*, Toronto: Mail Job Printing Co., 1895.

Fraser, Charles Ian, *The Clan Fraser of Lovat*, Edinburgh: W & A K Johnston Limited, 1952.

Fraser, David, *The Christian Watt Papers*, Edinburgh: Paul Harris Publishing, 1983.

Fraser, James, Rev., *The Wardlaw MS*, Scottish History Society, 1905.

Fraser, Simon, 17th Lord Lovat, *March Past; A Memoir*, London: George Weidenfeld & Nicolson Limited, 1978.

Harper, J. Ralph, *The Fraser Highlanders*, Montreal, Quebec: The David M. Stewart Museum, 1979, Reprint with index 1995.

Macdonald, Archibald, Rev. *The Old Lords of Lovat and Beaufort*, Inverness: The Northern Chronicle, 1934.

Mackenzie, Alexander, *History of the Frasers of Lovat*,* Inverness: A & W Mackenzie, 1896.

Maclean, Fitzroy, *Highlanders, A History of the Scottish Clans*, London: David Campbell Publishers Ltd., 1995.

Rannie, William F., *Clan Fraser; The Chief is a Lady*, Lincoln, Ontario, 1980.

Smiley, Lavinia, *The Frasers of Castle Fraser*, Salisbury, Wiltshire: Michael Russell (Publishing) Ltd., 1988.

Warrand, Duncan, *Some Fraser Pedigrees*, Inverness: Robert Carruthers & Sons, 1934.

Way, George and Romilly Squire, *Scottish Clans & Family Encyclopedia*, Glasgow: HarperCollins Publishers, 1994.

*Statements in this work should be treated with reserve until confirmed elsewhere

Other books by Lady Saltoun

Lady Saltoun's Favourite Fish Dishes

Wonderful recipes using a wide variety of fish and shellfish

Lady Saltoun's Favourite Puddings

Mouthwatering puddings for all occasions throughout the year

Prices (inclusive of postage & packing):

	Fish	*Puddings*
U.K.	£6.10	£7.10
Surface worldwide	£6.70	£7.70
Airmail Europe	£6.90	£7.90
Airmail Canada	£8.10	£9.10
Airmail USA	£8.10	£9.10
Airmail Australia	£8.60	£9.60

Both books available by mail order direct from ~

John Trail Ltd, 9 Mid Street,
Fraserburgh AB43 5AJ, Scotland